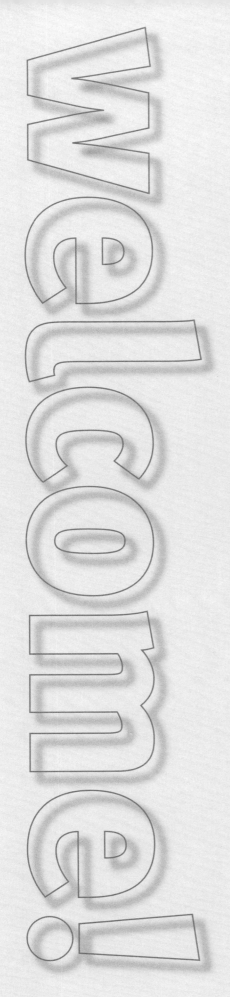

This is the 78th edition of *Books for the Teen Age*. It is a booklist created for you.
The cover art, featuring a photo collage of friends in New York City, invites you to visit our world of new ideas and possibilities. You will find stories of urban teens, classic stories revisited, graphic novels, memoirs of notable individuals, as well as books that will assist you in navigating through life.

We have a new look this year that features book reviews by New York City teens as well as interviews by teens with some of today's most exciting authors. There are many new categories for fiction and non-fiction titles. We hope these new categories will make your search for just the right book easier and more exciting.

The books on the list are available at Nathan Straus Teen Central, Donnell Library Center, 20 West 53rd Street, 212.621.0633, and at the branches of The New York Public Library. Each branch has a representative sampling of the books on this list and other books of special interest to teenagers. Many of the titles listed are available in recorded, Braille, or large-print format from the Andrew Heiskell Braille and Talking Book Library, 40 West 20th Street. Telephone: 212.206.5400, TTY 212.206.5458; 24-hour voicemail, 212.206.5458. Email: ahlbph@nypl.org.

Because you vary so much in your interests, maturity, and reading ability, these books differ greatly in difficulty and depth. They may be shelved in various places in the Library.

Ask your librarian to help you find a book you are interested in reading. Let your librarian know whether you like it or not. We are interested in your opinions! Write to us at: teenlink@nypl.org. Your opinions and ideas help us in selecting books for Young Adult collections in branch libraries and in preparing booklists for you.

Please visit us online: teenlink.nypl.org, where you will find additional booklists, special events for teens, opportunities to publish your poetry, stories, and essays online, audio excerpts from young adult novels, podcasts featuring local teens, and much more!

Got questions about homework? Check out: homeworkNYC.org

Sandra Payne

Sandra Payne
Coordinator of Young Adult Services

true lies
so unreal

Chick Lit

Barnholdt, Lauren
Reality Chick
Simon Pulse
Ally's freshman year
on film

Brian, Kate
Sweet 16
Simon & Schuster
Teagan finally seeing the
errors of her wrongs

Cabot, Meg
How to Be Popular
HarperTempest
One cherry super-big-gulp
mess=loserville

Castellucci, Cecil
The Queen of Cool
Candlewick
Libby's swift transforma-
tion from snotty to sweet

Cohn, Rachel
Two Steps Forward
Simon & Schuster
NYC fashionista girl,
determined to hate LA

Douglas, Lola
**True Confessions of a
Hollywood Starlet**
Razorbill
Out of rehab, incognito
in Indiana

Griffin, Adele
My Almost Epic Summer
Putnam's
Irene, surviving trashy
blogs and her nemesis' ex

Hollyer, Belinda, editor
You're the Best!
Kingfisher
New friends, old friends,
loving, hating

Myracle, Lauren
ttfn
Amulet
mad maddie, SnowAngel,
zoegirl: im again

Pollack, Jenny
Klepto
Viking
Friendship found among
filched fashions

Roberts, Laura Peyton
Queen B
Delacorte
Cassie striving to reach
new social heights

Ruby, Laura
Good Girls
HarperTempest
Audrey, going down in cell
phone photo history

Schorr, Melissa
Goy Crazy
Hyperion
Rachel falling for a super
sexy Catholic boy

Shepard, Sara
Pretty Little Liars
HarperTempest
Life-threatening text-
messages from
beyond the grave

Valdes-Rodriguez, Alisa
Haters
Little, Brown
Paski: face to face with
extreme culture shock

Walde, Christine
The Candy Darlings
Graphia
Friendship with a sugary
kiss

Wallington, Aury
Pop!
Razorbill
Doing the deed with her
best friend

Williams, Sheila
Girls Most Likely
One World
The geek, the beauty, the
voice, the perfectionist

Do-Overs

Cabot, Meg
Avalon High
HarperCollins
King Arthur's court in
modern-day Maryland

Geras, Adèle
Ithaka
Harcourt
A queen awaiting her
husband's return

Hunt, Scott, illustrator
Twice Told
Dutton
Original stories,
original art

Johnson, Maureen
Devilish
Razorbill
Selling their souls to a
cupcake-eating demon

Klein, Lisa
Ophelia
Bloomsbury
Captivated by dark-
haired Hamlet

Levithan, David
Marly's Ghost
Dial
Ben: Bah, humbug to
Valentine's Day

Lockhart, E.
Fly on the Wall
Delacorte
Gretchen going Kafka in
the boys' locker room

McCaughrean, Geraldine
Cyrano
Harcourt
Master swordsman,
brilliant wit, big nose

Sachs, Marilyn
First Impressions
Roaring Brook
A Pride and Prejudice
romantic switcheroo

Dudes, Punks, Playas, Guys, Etc.

Bondoux, Anne-Laure
The Killer's Tears
Delacorte
Paolo's new life with his
parents' murderer

Bradman, Tony, editor
My Dad's a Punk
Kingfisher
The ins and outs of
understanding your pops

Johnson, Henry and Paul
Hoppe
**Travis and Freddy's
Adventures in Vegas**
Dutton
Unstoppable duo's
journey to Sin City

Lyga, Barry
**The Astonishing
Adventures of Fanboy
& Goth Girl**
Houghton Mifflin
Loves comics, hates
high school

interview

Members of the Seward Park Branch Library's Teen Advisory Group offer questions via Email to Ned Vizzini, the author of *It's Kind of a Funny Story.*

How did you come up with the title *It's Kind of a Funny Story*, and were there any other titles that you thought of using?
I thought of the title *It's Kind of a Funny Story* while in the shower, when I was about 1/2 of the way through writing it. I had some other titles kicking around prior to that one but I thought it was really perfect. It was a phrase that I'd had in mind for a while—I think it's something we all say. "Listen, it's kind of a funny story..." The working title for *It's Kind of a Funny Story* before I came up with the real title halfway through was I Am a Triumph. (I'm really ashamed of it now, but I have to be honest.)

Did you decide to write *It's Kind of a Funny Story* because you spent time in a psychiatric hospital?
I wrote it because I went through an intense moment—call it a crucible—in my life. I had dealt with this depression for two years and when it finally came to a head and I got into and out of the hospital, I finally had something to write that was worth reading.

Was this book painful for you to write?
It was difficult for me to write *It's Kind of a Funny Story* even though it only took about a month. For some reason, I remember a lot of sweating. It was a lot of waking up, writing, driving myself, sweating, sleeping, waking, writing, listening to John Coltrane "A Love Supreme"... it was a tough but ultimately cosmic experience.

Where did you come up with the idea of *Tentacles and Anchors*?
Even when I was a kid, I remember being conscious of tasks piling up around me. Homework and chores and phone calls. Then email came and then I became a professional writer and the tasks got more and more STUCK in me and I started thinking I could never break free—I called them "tentacles." "Anchors" just came out as I was writing *It's Kind of a Funny Story* as the opposite of tentacles. I didn't spend a lot of time thinking up either of these terms—they just showed up in the book.

Did you like drawing maps when you were growing up?
I LOVED maps when I was growing up. I didn't draw any maps when I was in the psych hospital, though, but I DID do some art while I was there, visible at http://www.nedvizzini.com/writing/. From the ages of 6 – 12 I made maps just like Craig, and I never finished them just like Craig.

Was writing this book a therapeutic experience for you?
Writing *It's Kind of a Funny Story* was more than a therapeutic experience. I would call it a transcendent experience—I felt like it brought me to another place. I'm much, much better now.

Of the books you've written, which one do you like best?
I think *It's Kind of a Funny Story* is my best book. I would hope that the latest would be the best—that means I'm getting better as a writer!

What made you or, rather, inspired you to start writing?
When I was in 2nd grade, the school year started and in addition to English and math, we had a special class called "Writer's Workshop." They gave you a blank book to fill and I just went off putting stories inside. I couldn't believe it was a class! Then, when I was 12, I read George Orwell's essay "Such, Such Were the Joys" and it made me want to write about my own life. Then, when I was a freshman in high school, I started reading an alternative newspaper called *New York Press* and the fearlessness of the writers therein provided the final spark.

What was it like to be published as a teenager? Do you have any advice for aspiring teen authors?
There is an article online about my experience being published as a teenager (http://www.villagevoice.com/arts/0646,wigginton,75019,12.html). It was an honor, obviously, but it brought with it a lot of pressure. When you start young, people tend to assume that you're a flash-in-the-pan who won't maintain your success. At the same time, there are people who don't like you very much because you've done at 19 what took them 30 or 40 years. Then, there's the added worry that if your books don't sell, people will say that you're not very talented and you just got the chance to publish because you were young. So those are the negatives. But all in all, I've had an amazing life and the day I first saw my name in *New York Press* was a day that pretty much fulfilled all my dreams. (Everything else has been gravy.)

As for aspiring teen authors: the key is, don't write a book. Especially if you're young, you're not going to have the discipline to follow through on a complete work of fiction, which has to be on your mind all the time for months. Also don't write poetry or short stories, unless you've got one really good short story—there's not much of a market for that. Cut your teeth writing for newspapers and magazines. The key here is this:

At the front of every newspaper and magazine in America (sometimes on page 2 or 3) is something called a masthead. The masthead lists the names and occupations of all the writers/artists/editors who work for the paper. At the bottom of the masthead is an address called the slush mail address. You will probably see it in tiny letters down there and really have to struggle to read it. This is the address that unknown writers can send their work to!

Whatever you enjoy reading, you should send your writing to. If you like cars, send to *Road and Track*. If you've got a crazy story about homeless people or music, look for a local alternative paper in your city (like *New York Press*, it'll come out every week and have listings for all the concerts/parties going on); you will, at least, get a response and get an idea how good your stuff is.

It's Kind of a Funny Story is published by Miramax Books/Hyperion.

Visit Ned Vizzini online: www.nedvizzini.com

Book Excerpt:
It's so hard to talk when you want to kill yourself. That's above and beyond everything else, and it's not a mental complaint—it's a physical thing, like it's physically hard to open your mouth and make the words come out. They don't come out smooth and in conjunction with your brain the way normal people's words do; they come out in chunks as if from a crushed-ice dispenser; you stumble on them as they gather behind your lower lip, So you just keep quiet.

3

Portman, Frank
King Dork
Delacorte
Solving his father's murder with Catcher in the Rye

Rosoff, Meg
Just in Case
Wendy Lamb
15-year-old basketcase running from fate

Simmons, Michael
Vandal
Roaring Brook
Will's brother Jason-violently out of control

Sonnenblick, Jordan
Notes from the Midnight Driver
Scholastic
The perils of killing a garden gnome

Trottier, Maxine
Three Songs for Courage
Tundra
Great car, beautiful girlfriend, bent on revenge

Trueman, Terry
No Right Turn
HarperTempest
Reclaiming his mojo *with a '76 Corvette*

Vizzini, Ned
It's Kind of a Funny Story
Miramax
Craig: stressed out and determined to live for real

Get Me Outta This Place

Fletcher, Christine
Tallulah Falls
Bloomsbury
Stranded in rural Tennessee

Garden, Nancy
Endgame
Harcourt
Gray, doing time for a violent crime

Hernández, Jo Ann Yolanda
The Throwaway Piece
Piñata
Jewel, the state kid, stuck in the system

Love, D. Anne
Semiprecious
Margaret K. McElderry
Trapped, tormented and teased in the middle of Texas

Lowell, Pamela
Returnable Girl
Marshall Cavendish
Ronnie, the foster home reject

Meehl, Brian
Out of Patience
Delacorte
Jake, cursed forever to stay in toilet town

Pinder, Margaret
But I Don't Want to Be a Movie Star
Dutton
Escaping the lap of luxury

Van Draanen, Wendelin
Runaway
Knopf
Holly on her own, chronicling her survival

Waite, Judy
Forbidden
Atheneum
Aching for contact in the outside world

God Only Knows

Cheripko, Jan
sun moon stars rain
Front Street
A college dropout de-puzzling his life

Cooney, Caroline B.
A Friend at Midnight
Delacorte
Questioning her faith when her brother is abandoned

Johnston, Julie
A Very Fine Line
Tundra
Rosalind, discovering powers of clairvoyance

Lynch, Chris
Sins of the Fathers
HarperTempest
Three friends, one cold Catholic school winter

MacLean, Christine Kole
How It's Done
Flux
Grace breaking free from her strict father's grasp

Reinhardt, Dana
A Brief Chapter in My Impossible Life
Wendy Lamb
Simone's adopted present vs. her biological past

Wittlinger, Ellen
Blind Faith
Simon & Schuster
Liz and Nathan coping together in the wake of loss

Hookups, Heartaches, True Love

Barnes, Derrick
The Making of Dr. Truelove
Simon Pulse
Diego, the 16-year-old online Dr. Feelgood

Cohn, Rachel and David Levithan
Nick & Norah's Infinite Playlist
Knopf
Turbulent love set to the beat of punk rock

Colasanti, Susane
When It Happens
Viking
Slacker rock star falling for the class brainiac

Conway, Celeste
The Melting Season
Delacorte
Giselle-on her toes, in love on the streets of NYC

Dessen, Sarah
Just Listen
Viking
Annabel meeting the guy with the coolest iPod ever

Dower, Laura
Rewind
Point
Hope, Lucas, Cady: getting played in reverse

Jenkins, A.M.
Beating Heart
HarperCollins
Love and lust among the living and the dead

Miller, Sarah
Inside the Mind of Gideon Rayburn
St. Martin's
Reading the thoughts of the one you love

interview

Members of the Jefferson Market Branch Library and the Tompkins Square Branch Library's Teen Advisory Groups offer questions via Email to Rachel Cohn and David Levithan, the co-authors of *Nick & Norah's Infinite Playlist*.

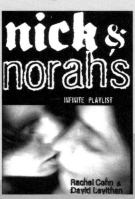

Book Excerpt:
And I can't stand the thought of it. I see it all unfolding and I know I have to do something — anything—to stop it.

So I, this random bassist in an average queercore band, turn to this girl in flannel who I don't even know and say:

"I know this is going to sound strange, but would you mind being my girlfriend for the next five minutes?"

How did you come up with the idea for the story and the idea for team-writing the book?
Rachel: I was taking a walk around the reservoir in Central Park and thinking about the Thin Man movies from the 1930s (which featured a husband-and-wife team of bantering socialite-detectives named Nick & Nora Charles) and I had the random thought that it would be fun to update those names within a YA context. Only I figured I needed a guy to write the Nick perspective 'cuz what do I know about being a guy? Right, nothing. David happened to be pretty much the only guy YA writer I knew at that time so I pitched the idea to him and he was game for it. While I had two character names and a basic premise in mind, he actually had a story to develop for them, so it worked out nicely and symbiotically from the very beginning.

What were your inspirations for the characters of *Nick and Norah*? Are they similar to you? How did you come up with their names?
David: For me, the inspiration for Nick was the moment I realized he was the straight bass player in a queercore band. I have no idea where that particular idea came from, but the moment I had it, I knew exactly where the book would start—with him on stage, having an ex-related meltdown. The name was of Rachel's devising...

Rachel: The names Nick & Norah (with an "h") were inspired by Nick & Nora Charles from the Thin Man movies, and NOT by the Nick & Nora pajama brand (also inspired by the Thin Man movies), which I've been asked a lot! I should be a good author and point out the Thin Man movies were based on books by Dashiell Hammett but being a bad author, I have never read those books. As for Norah's character, she's a little bit inspired by my sister Martha, who's now 19, and is very cool and hip and music-obsessed, and Norah also has some of the brashness mixed with insecurity that I remember from being Norah's age.

What was the system for writing the book? Did you know what the other person was writing or was it a surprise when you got it? Were you ever shocked by what the other person wrote?
David: Rachel and I each sat in isolation booths, not unlike those in 1950s quiz shows. But seriously...we were, by happenstance, on separate coasts at the time. I wrote

the first chapter, emailed it to Rachel, then received the second chapter from her and started writing the third. We didn't plan anything ahead of time, so there were many, many surprises. But that's what kept it interesting.

Rachel: For instance, I continue to be surprised that David can pull words like "happenstance" out of his bag of tricks. It's never not interesting, writing with him. If only he'd finally let me out of my isolation chamber! (Someone, please help me!)

You totally made the club scene of the Lower East Side and East Village come alive. What influenced your decision to set the story in those neighborhoods? Did you have to do any research? Have you ever gone to clubs like the ones featured in the book?
David: It was Rachel's idea to have Nick and Norah both be bridge-and-tunnel kids, and once Nick was in the queercore scene, there weren't many other places they could be. I mean, it would be interesting to imagine a queercore club in Times Square, or the Upper East Side... but that didn't quite strike me as true. So we started on the Lower East Side and went from there. The clubs are based on real clubs, but we changed the identities to protect the innocent. Or, in some cases, the guilty.

Music is such a huge part of the book. How did you decide what kind of music and bands that characters liked? Is the kind of music you like the same kind of music that Nick and Norah like?
Rachel: Along with Nick & Norah, I think it's safe to say that David and I both live and breathe by music (and our iPods), so giving that quality to the characters was second nature. Each song reference and band name was very carefully picked. We tried to use music references that would stand the test of time—either because the songs or bands were that good...or just that bad. We gave up several references to songs and bands we thought nobody would remember in the long run.

What did you learn about each other and each other's writing style while writing the book?
David: Well, we certainly learned how well our styles mixed together.

Rachel: I learned that David can write a nearly perfect, fully-formed chapter within a matter of hours (envy), and that he is very particular about his shirts.

Will you write another book together? Will there be a sequel to Nick and Norah?
David: We were going to do a sequel, but then we realized it had the same exact plot as *Dreamgirls*. So instead we focused on another book – *Naomi & Ely's No Kiss List*, which will be out in August.

Nick & Norah's Infinite Playlist is published by Alfred A. Knopf, an imprint of Random House, a division of Random House, Inc.

Visit Rachel Cohn online: www.rachelcohn.com
Visit David Levithan online: www.davidlevithan.com

interview

Charisse Campbell, a member of the West New Brighton Branch Library's Teen Advisory Group, offers questions via Email to Walter Dean Myers, the author of *Street Love*.

Book Excerpt:
Their tribe is the more familiar
We have seen them on every corner
Of every city in America.
They make us walk
Faster. They make us think of locked doors.
Of differences we would like to deny.

How can you or someone you know relate to the character Damien?
I can just look at my two sons, Michael and Chris. They are both like Damien.

What do you want readers to get from reading this novel?
I want them to enjoy the book and to think about how these young people make very important choices.

Why did you decide this story was going to be written in poem narrative format?
The format made the book a more interesting challenge for me. I love to work with language and see how many ways I can express the inner feelings of my characters.

Chico and Sledge are troublemakers; are there any good qualities in them?
Chico and Sledge are all right. They're challenging Damien because they have doubts about their own futures. Challenges are good, although sometimes troublesome. We need to respond in a positive manner to all the Chicos and Sledges in the world.

What made you decide to write this story about Harlem?
Two reasons: I'm from Harlem is the first. The second is that Harlem, for me, represents all of the inner cities in the country.

When people hear of Harlem, they think about gangs, killing and drama. How have you changed people's perspective in *Street Love*?
I want people to think of Harlem as a community with real people who have feelings and emotions and the courage to deal with adversity.

A lot of teenagers my age love books that rhyme. This story has this flow; was it your intent to write the story this way or did it just pop out?
Actually, I worked very hard to give the characters different speech rhythms, and to vary the rhyme schemes.

What advice would you give readers who are experiencing the same issues Damien and Junice are going through?
I received advice from a group of teenaged girls in Chicago. They told me that the young couple needed to understand their legal rights, the risks they're taking, and to talk to family members when possible.

This writing in this book is different from all your other books. Why?
Writing is such a pleasure for me I want to do it in as many ways as possible. Also, I wanted to bring my best writing to this difficult situation.

If you had to pick your favorite character, who would it be?
I love Junice.

Were there any limitations when writing this story?
I wasn't given any restrictions by my publisher.

Would you consider making this book into a play or movie?
If anyone's interested, give me a call!

Why did you decide to create a character like Junice?
I spend a lot of time at trials. I watched as a woman was being sentenced and then led, sobbing, from the courtroom. But I also saw her children sitting with the spectators and my heart went out to them. In thinking what they would do, and how they would survive, Junice was created.

Why is it that the fathers of the main characters (Junice and Damien) aren't mentioned a lot through the story?
Damien's mother is just more aggressive in what she wants for her son. Junice's father has never been in her life.

Is it ironic that Damien likes a girl like Junice when he can have a girl like Roxanne?
I think young people have very difficult choices to make in their lives. Junice chooses to assume the burden of protecting her Melissa. Damien chooses to both understand what Junice is going through and to become part of that struggle.

Thanks for your great questions!

Street Love is published by Amistad-HarperTempest, an imprint of HarperCollins Publishers.

Visit Walter Dean Myers online:
www.walterdeanmyersbooks.com

Myers, Walter Dean
Street Love
Amistad/Harper Tempest
Damien & Junice:
Star-crossed in Harlem

Just My Opinion!

Street Love is about two teenagers from two different worlds. Junice is a dark-skinned girl about sixteen years of age who has to take on a motherly role at a young age. Her mother goes to jail for selling drugs. It's up to Rachel Davis (Department of Family Services) to decide if she should stay with her grandmother. Damien comes from a family who has money. His mother wants to protect him from the streets and anybody who isn't on her level. She feels that because they have money, they should let everyone know that he is the complete opposite. Damien is attracted to Junice because he sees her pain and wants to console her. I really enjoyed this book. It's very different from how Walter Dean Myers usually writes. The words rhyme and it has this flow that makes the story come to life. This book is great!
Teen Reviewer:
Charisse Campbell
West New Brighton
Branch, Staten Island

Namioka, Lensey
Mismatch
Delacorte
Sue and Andy more than just chopsticks and rice

Nelson, Blake
Prom Anonymous
Viking
Love! Dating! Prom!
Stress!

Shaw, Tucker
The Hookup Artist
HarperCollins
Lucas: finding a guy for everyone but himself

Shulman, Polly
Enthusiasm
Putnam's
Austen-crazed Ashleigh on a quest for romance

Soto, Gary
Accidental Love
Harcourt
Falling for a nerd with bad taste in socks

Stone, Tanya Lee
A Bad Boy Can Be Good for a Girl
Wendy Lamb
A player's conquests scrawled on the bathroom wall

Vail, Rachel
You, Maybe
HarperCollins
Josie, fierce, independent and falling for a senior

Just My Opinion!

The book [You, Maybe] is about an ordinary girl that spends her time talking about philosophy. Josie is an independent girl that doesn't care about what boys think about...well that was until she started hooking up with the hottest senior at her high school. What first began as a game ended in love for Josie. I like this book because of all the stages that Josie had to pass through with her new boyfriend.
Teen Reviewer:
Mayte Gonzales
Riverside Branch Library,
Manhattan

Liars

Dorfman, Joaquin
Playing It Cool
Random House
Problem-solver Sebastian swapping identities

Headley, Justina Chen
Nothing but the Truth
Little, Brown
Patty: half Taiwanese, half white shipped off to summer camp

Just My Opinion!

Patty Ho is a half Asian and half white teenager who has a hard time accepting who she is. She has a future planned out for her by everyone but herself. She must overcome being different from everyone else and must learn to fit comfortably in her own skin and escape the prejudices of society. Patty has a hard time characterizing who she really is. This is a problem most teens in today's society must overcome. I like this book because it helps teens, like myself, overcome society's view of an ideal person. It teaches each person to be comfortable in their own skin and reach their ideal beauty. This novel uses an insight view of a teenager who is overcome with feeling different and must learn how to empower herself. I would recommend this book to every teenager who wants to learn to feel comfortable in his or her own skin and learn to accept who she or he really is.
Teen Reviewer:
Alexis Savaterre
Richmondtown
Branch Library,
Staten Island

James, Brian
Dirty Liar
PUSH
Benji: leaving everything behind, trying not to self-destruct

Na, An
Wait for Me
Putnam's
Mina, creating the illusion of perfection

Nelson, Blake
Paranoid Park
Viking
Skater-punk wannabe hiding a grisly murder

Steele, J. M.
The Taker
Hyperion
Aching to escape the confines of the SAT

Novels in Verse

Block, Francesca Lia
Psyche in a Dress
Joanna Cotler
Love myth updated for a new age

Frost, Helen
The Braid
Francis Foster
Two sisters, two countries, new lives

Herrick, Steven
By the River
Front Street
Harry, yearning for a bigger life

Hopkins, Ellen
Burned
Margaret K. McElderry
Pattyn spinning out of control in Nevada

Rylant, Cynthia
Ludie's Life
Harcourt
Growing up in the Appalachian mountains

Smith, Kirsten
The Geography of Girlhood
Little, Brown
The highs and the lows of becoming a woman

Parents from Hell

Dalton, Annie and Maria Dalton
Invisible Threads
Delacorte
Carrie Ann and Naomi: finding their mothers, finding themselves

Hurwin, Davida Wills
Circle the Soul Softly
HarperCollins
New school, glamorous life, recurring nightmares

MacCready, Robin Merrow
Buried
Dutton
Obsessive-compulsive Claudia going full-throttle

Marchetta, Melina
Looking for Alibrandi
Knopf
Nice guys, bad boys, missing dads

Paul, Dominique
The Possibility of Fireflies
Simon & Schuster
Ellie's mom taking a break from parenting

Werlin, Nancy
The Rules of Survival
Dial
Longing to escape the brutality of a volatile mother

Dead & Relatively Dead Relatives

Freymann-Weyr, Garret
Stay With Me
Houghton Mifflin
Leila, shattered by suicide, falling for an older man

Hacker, Randi
Life As I Knew It
Simon Pulse
Angelina, pre and post stroke

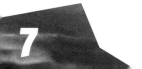

Jones, Kimberly K.
Sand Dollar Summer
Margaret K. McElderry
Recuperating on Maine's
sandy shores

MacCullough, Carolyn
Drawing the Ocean
Deborah Brodie
Haunted by the death
of her twin brother

Mass, Wendy
**Jeremy Fink and the
Meaning of Life**
Little, Brown
One locked box, one
long-kept secret

Oates, Joyce Carol
**After the Wreck, I Picked
Myself Up, Spread My
Wings, and Flew Away**
HarperTempest
Therapy, nightmares,
and a new appreciation
for painkillers

Runyon, Brent
Maybe
Knopf
Brian's grief pushed into
the passenger seat

Tolan, Stephanie S.
Listen!
HarperCollins
Friendship and healing
from a four-legged friend

Risky Business

Cart, Michael, editor
**Rush Hour, Volume 4,
Reckless**
Delacorte
Giving in to the
temptation

Gallo, Donald R., editor
What Are You Afraid Of?
Candlewick
10 fabulous, fearsome,
phobias

Just My Opinion!

This book [What Are You
Afraid Of?] *contains
stories about phobias.
From a boy who couldn't
speak to an audience to a
girl who just won't gain
weight. All these stories
are portrayed by teenage
characters and are well
written. Interesting book.*
Teen Reviewer:
Rosa Patricia Mateo
Kingsbridge Branch
Library, Bronx

Goobie, Beth
**The Dreams Where the
Losers Go**
Orca
Injuring herself to escape
abuse

Heggum, Lisa, editor
All Sleek and Skimming
Orca
Stories funny, playful,
nasty, heartbreaking

Hoffmann, Kerry Cohen
Easy
Simon & Schuster
Pain cooled by an older
man's touch

Lynn, Tracy
Rx
Simon Pulse
From the medicine
cabinet to the street

Rees, Celia
The Wish House
Candlewick
First fling, first love,
first death

Vrettos, Adrienne Maria
Skin
Margaret K. McElderry
Donnie's sister fading
away to nothing

Zarr, Sara
Story of a Girl
Little, Brown
Suffering from rumors
of slutdom

Road Trip!

Behrens, Andy
All the Way
Dutton
Driving 900 miles to
hookup

Budhos, Marina
Ask Me No Questions
Atheneum
Nadira's father arrested
and detained at the
border

Book Excerpt:
I remember when we first
arrived at the airport in
New York, how tight my
mother's hand felt in
mine. How her mouth
became stiff when the
uniformed man split open
the packing tape around
our suitcase and plunged
his hands into her
underwear and saris,
making us feel dirty
inside. Abba's leg was
jiggling a little, which is
what it does when he's
nervous. Even then we
were afraid because we
knew we were going to
stay past the date on the
little blue stamp of the
tourist visa in our
passports. Everyone does
it. You buy a fake social
security number for a few
hundred dollars and then
you can work. A lot of the
Bangladeshis here are
illegal, they say. Some
get lucky and win the
Diversity Lottery so they
can stay.

Cooney, Caroline B.
Hit The Road
Delacorte
On the lam with granny
and her friends

Cooper, Patrick
I Is Someone Else
Delacorte
A journey abroad to find
a lost brother

Ehrenhaft, Daniel
The After Life
Razorbill
Will, the drunkard druggie
driving down South

Gallo, Donald R., editor
Destination Unexpected
Candlewick
Excursions of discovery
inside and out

Green, John
**An Abundance of
Katherines**
Dutton
Colin, dumped 19 times
and on the road to
recovery

Book Excerpt:
But mostly for those
fourteen hours, he read
and reread Katherine
XIX's inscription:

Col,
Here's to all the places we
went. And all the places
we'll go. And here's
me, whispering again
and again and again
and again:
ilovevou.
yrs forever,
K-a-t-h-e- r-i-n-e

Eventually, he found his
bed too comfortable for
his state of mind, so he
lay down on his back, his
legs sprawled across the
carpet. He anagrammed
"yrs forever" until he
found one he liked: sorry
fever. And then he lay
there in his fever of sorry
and repeated the now
memorized note in his
head and wanted to cry,
but instead he only felt
this aching behind his
solar plexus. Crying adds
something: crying is you,
plus tears. But the feeling
Colin had was some
horrible opposite of
crying. It was you, minus
something. He kept
thinking about one
word—forever—and felt
the burning ache just
beneath his rib cage. It
hurt like the worst ass-
kicking he'd ever gotten.
And he'd gotten plenty.

Harmon, Michael
Skate
Knopf
On the run to find a father

Hemphill, Helen
Long Gone Daddy
Front Street
Harlan Q, his dad,
a body, $50,000

Lanagan, Margo
White Time
EOS
Worlds surreal, fantastic,
dark, hopeful

Mourlevat, Jean-Claude
The Pull of the Ocean
Delacorte
7 brothers escaping a
violent father

Reisz, Kristopher
Tripping to Somewhere
Simon Pulse
Outcasts leaving
everything they know
behind

Smith, Sherri L.
Sparrow
Delacorte
Kendall: orphaned,
alone, on the road

To Be Continued

Atwater-Rhodes, Amelia
Wolfcry
Delacorte
A shapeshifter's dilemma:
duty vs. love

Avi
**Crispin: at the Edge of
the World**
Hyperion
Learning who he is and
who to trust

Brian, Kate
Private
Simon Pulse
Reed, attending boarding
school, surviving mean
girls

Members of the Seward Park Branch Library's Teen Advisory Group offer questions via Email to John Green, the author of *An Abundance of Katherines*.

Not a question, just a note: we're jealous of your anagram skills. Here's a question: do you practice anagramming now that you've done writing *An Abundance of Katherines*? Did you write your own anagrams for Katherines yourself? (TWO questions!)
I'm really not very good at anagramming, but because I wanted the character in the book to be ridiculously good at it, I had to practice a lot. And I really believed that when I finished the book, I would never anagram ever again under any circumstances ever. And then, while I was on tour in Iowa, someone told me that Britney Spears anagrams to Presbyterians. And I immediately got back into anagramming, because sometimes it is just so awesome.

What's your favorite novel that you've written?
I hate to choose between the two, because then the other one will be all sad, and the whole thing will be sort of Velveteen Rabbit-ey. So I'll say what my parents always told my brother and me: I love them both—equally but different.

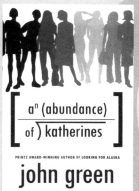

What inspired you to write *An Abundance of Katherines*?
Two things, really: I wanted to write about a guy who is going through an extreme case of that horrible process wherein we realize that we are not quite so unique as we always hoped (that is, real people are more like Weasleys than Potters). And also, I wanted to write a book with a Muslim guy who was religious but generally pretty normal, like all the Muslim guys I know.

Who is Alaska based on?
As a character, she is based on a lot of people I knew in high school and since (and, to an extent, my high-school self). But the relationship that Pudge has with Alaska—the way he romanticizes her and sees her as this larger-than-life force of nature—is very much based on the way I felt about this one girl in high school. But I can't tell you her name, because she still doesn't know I ever had a crush on her, and I'm keeping it that way.

Can you write a book about medieval times?
I might, but I don't think I will in the near future. I really admire people who write about medieval times, because 1. it is really hard to remember how to spell medieval, and 2. you have to do so much research, and 3. you have to constantly remember that no one in medieval times ever took baths or brushed their teeth, so everything smelled absolutely rancid. Doing that much research, and thinking about their teeth—it's too much for me at this point in my writing life.

Have you been dumped 19 times like Colin in *An Abundance of Katherines*?
I've been dumped way, way, way more times than Colin. (53, to be exact.) But I was never dumped by a Katherine. Or 19 people of any name, actually, although there were several Marys.

Do you have advice for teens that get dumped?
Well, I think the advice that Hassan gives Colin is excellent: Dumpees must never, ever, ever call the Dumpers, no matter how badly every cell in your body screams out to talk to your Dumper. It's like picking a scab: It will only slow the healing process, and it could possibly lead to infection.

Also, I think it is important to remember that in the long run—in the very, very, very long run—getting dumped can be a good thing. I had an ex-girlfriend once who told me something quite smart right after she dumped me. She said, "John, every relationship you ever have is going to end in break-up. Except one." Seen in that context, you can always just say, "Well, I guess that wasn't the one."

What new book are you working on?
I don't know what it's called yet even though I'm about two thirds finished with it, but my new book is about a girl who disappears after an all-night adventure, and the guy who tries to track her down across the country.

Will any of your books be made into movies? Which book (in your opinion) would make the best movie?
Looking for Alaska is being developed as a movie by Paramount with Josh Schwartz (who created "The O.C.") writing and directing. It's been a lot of fun to work with them on the movie, and I'm hopeful that they'll make it and that it will be good. But I still think *Katherines* could be a hilarious movie—we'll see.

What are some of your favorite books?
Oh, I have so many. Just a few I think my readers might like: *The Virgin Suicides*, by Jeffrey Euginedes; *The Amazing Adventures of Kavalier and Clay*, by Michael Chabon; *The Book Thief*, by Markus Zusak; *Their Eyes Were Watching God*, by Zora Neale Hurston; *Song of Solomon*, by Toni Morrison; *The Realm of Possibility*, by David Levithan; and *All the King's Men*, by Robert Penn Warren. Boy, that's a weird list.

Is John Green your real name?
Yes. If I were to come up with a pseudonym, I would think of something more creative.

Where do you live (we will not stalk you)?
I live on the Upper West Side of Manhattan.

Will you give us all $100?
That question is grammatically ambiguous. Are you asking whether I will give each of you $100, or are you asking whether I will you all, as a collective, a total of $100? In either case, the answer is no. But it's not that I don't love you! It's just like my mom always used to say when I asked her for five dollars: "If I give you five dollars, how are you going to learn what five dollars is worth?" It never even crossed my mind to ask for $100. But I guess this is New York. Everything's more expensive here.

Thanks for the great questions—I feel fortunate to have such smart and thoughtful and funny readers.

An Abundance of Katherines is published by Dutton Books a member of Penguin Group (USA) Inc.

Visit John Green online: www.sparksflyup.com

Colfer, Eoin
**Artemis Fowl:
The Lost Colony**
Miramax
Ancient secrets of
the fairy world

Haddix, Margaret
Peterson
Among the Free
Simon & Schuster
Luke, overthrowing
the population police

Jacques, Brian
Voyage of Slaves
Philomel
A boy and his dog fighting
evil on the high seas

Manning, Sarra
French Kiss
Speak
Falling in love with
a guy every girl wants

McCaffrey, Anne and
Todd McCaffrey
Dragon's Fire
Del Rey
Defending Pern from
destruction

Nix, Garth
Sir Thursday
Scholastic
Fighting a war before
returning to earth

Novik, Naomi
His Majesty's Dragon
Del Rey
A British soldier's
precious bounty

Reeve, Philip
Infernal Devices
EOS
Desire for adventure
leads to tragedy

Richardson, V. A.
**The Moneylender's
Daughter**
Bloomsbury
Adam and Jade torn
between loyalty and love

Scott, Manda
Boudica
Bantam Dell
Brutal Celtic queen
preparing for war

Shusterman, Neal
Duckling Ugly
Dutton
The chance to trade
in your face

Skurzynski, Gloria
The Choice
Atheneum
Stay in paradise or battle
a dictator

Sniegoski, Tom
Sleeper Code
Razorbill
Teenager or assassin,
two minds, one body

Stroud, Jonathan
Ptolemy's Gate
Miramax
Three destinies converge

Westerfeld, Scott
Blue Noon
EOS
Showdown with
the Farklings

Westerfeld, Scott
Specials
Simon Pulse
Keeping Uglies down
and Pretties stupid

Just My Opinion!
This book [Specials] *is
about Tally and how she
is now, a special kind of
like a secret agent for her
city. One of her friends
was kidnapped and she
not only has to save him,
but she also gets rid of an
organization threatening
the cities around the
world. I thought this book
was extremely good
and addicting. I kept on
reading it on and on.
I loved every bit of it. It
was amazing!!!!!!!! My
whole class is waiting
to read this book! Yeah!*
Teen Reviewer:
Ilham Elkatani
Bronx Library Center,
Bronx

Wilcox, Mary
Backstage Pass
Delacorte
Star-struck sisters, top-
rated sitcom, tabloids

What's So
Funny?

Banks, Steven
King of the Creeps
Knopf
Looks like Bob Dylan,
only knows one chord

Caires, Steven
The Joys of Engrish
Tarcher/Penguin
Lost in translation???

Carney, Charles
The Acme Catalog
Chronicle
Fake holes, giant
magnets, iron birdseed
and more

Carney, Jeff
**The Adventures of
Michael MacInnes**
Farrar Straus and Giroux
Mucking with the wrong
side of authority

Charles B. Anderson
Design Company and
Michael Nelson
**Fluffy Humpy Poopy
Puppy**
Abrams Image
Snarky, snoopy, campy,
canines

Defoe, Gideon
The Pirates!
Vintage
Kicking arse in the sea
shanty life

Garza, Mario
Stuff on My Cat
Chronicle
A fierce frenzy of frocked
felines

Korman, Gordon
Born to Rock
Hyperion
Leo hanging with his
punk rock pop

Masyga, Mark
Peeps
Abrams Image
Living the sweet life,
the sugar-coated truth

Pratchett, Terry
Johnny and the Dead
HarperCollins
Saving the cemetery
with the dearly departed

Shields, Gillian
**The Actual Real Reality
of Jennifer James**
Katherine Tegen
1 heroine, 1 prize, 1000
complications

Voigt, Cynthia
**Bad Girls, Bad Girls,
Whatcha Gonna Do?**
Atheneum
Mikey + Margalo = 9th
grade mischief

Word on
the Street

Booth, Coe
Tyrell
PUSH
Stuck in a shelter,
aching for a break,
keeping it legit

Just My Opinion!
This book [Tyrell] *is about
a boy named Tyrell. He is
forced to become a man
at a young age. Since his
mom doesn't give a damn
about him or his little
brother and his father
(who really cares) is in
jail. My favorite part of
the book is when he finds
out that his girlfriend
wasn't a virgin and he
thought that once they
got married that he would
be the only one who
would have been with her.*
Teen Reviewer:
Tamar Charles
Wakefield Branch Library,
Bronx

This book [Tyrell] *is about
a boy named Tyrell. His
father got sent to jail
because he was selling
drugs and now it's up to
him to be a man and care
for his family but he don't
wanna sell drugs and end
up like his father so he
tries things like swiping
Metro Cards for people
for a dollar just to get
food to eat and his mom
and little bro are in a
roach-infested motel.
I like the book because
it's good to read about
how a young boy is
struggling for his family.*
Teen Reviewer:
Jasmine Howard
Wakefield Branch Library,
Bronx

WOW! This book [Tyrell] *is
great. It's one of the best
books I've read, so far.
The part I liked most
about this book was that
Tyrell sacrificed his
freedom to support his
family and he knows how
to deal with his struggle.*
Teen Reviewer:
Jose Ventura
Bronx Library Center,
Bronx

Bowsher, Melodie
My Lost and Found Life
Bloomsbury
Ashley: desperate and
about to lose everything

Going, K.L.
Saint Iggy
Harcourt
Kicked out of high school,
surviving on the streets

McDonald, Janet
Harlem Hustle
Frances Foster
Eric, abandoned and
struggling for hip-hop
stardom

Pagliarulo, Antonio
A Different Kind of Heat
Delacorte
Luz, consumed by rage,
bent on revenge

interview

Members of the Wakefield Branch Library's Teen Advisory Group offer questions via Email to Coe Booth the author of *Tyrell*.

Do you take people you know and just change the names to make your characters? They're so real!
Thanks for saying my characters are real, but no, I don't base them on real people. I don't think my friends would like that very much! Sometimes I make my characters do little things that are based on real people, though. For example, when I was a teenager, a friend of mine had a little Virgin Mary statue in his car and he used to turn it around whenever he kissed his girlfriend. So I took that little bit and used it to add some reality to Novisha's personality.

But for the most part, I just make my characters up from scratch. That's part of the fun of being a fiction writer. You can create people and then follow them around to see what they're going to do next! It's like playing The Sims, only much, much better!

How did you make Tyrell speak and act like a real guy? He's like all the guys at my school, but he's not real.
To be honest, I was kind of worried about writing a whole book from the point of view of a boy. I kept asking myself, "What do I know about being a guy?" But once I started writing the first chapter, this boy's voice just started flowing from me and it was really kind of fun! It's interesting trying to see the world from the perspective of the opposite sex. Immediately after writing the first page, I really started to like Tyrell and I wanted to figure out what he was all about. Sometimes I would write a scene and have to throw it away because I was getting in Tyrell's way and trying to solve his problems in my own "girly" way. Things worked out a whole lot better when I tapped into my "inner guy" and let him solve things in his own unique style.

How could I get my own stories published? I write a lot in my journal, but don't know what to do after that.
If you're in middle school or high school, I think you should read everything you can get your hands on and write for fun. These are the years where you can get better at writing and find out exactly what kind of writing you want to do. There are places on the Internet especially designed for teenagers where you can publish short work, too. Another thing you can think about now is creating a blog or a MySpace page to publish your short stories and poetry.

If you're really serious about being published, the first thing I recommend is learning as much as possible about the publishing world. Figure out who publishes the kind of writing you do and how you should go about contacting magazine editors. If you want to have a book published, you need to write the whole thing first. Then you should get a literary agent to help find the right editor for you. It can be a long process sometimes, so you need to be patient. But if you've worked hard on being the best writer you can be, your writing will hopefully find a home somewhere!

Book Excerpt:
My seven-year-old brother, Troy, is playing with my basketball out in front of the building, throwing it up against the wall and catching it like it's summer out here. My moms is outside too, leaning against a van, smoking with some other woman. All our stuff is packed up in one tore up black suitcase and two garbage bags on the ground by my moms. I wanna ask her if they found us a place, but I just glare at her and walk by without saying a word. I don't got nothing to say to her no more.

Did you grow up like Tyrell did? Is that where you get your ideas?
No, I didn't grow up anything like Tyrell. I'm from the Bronx, but I didn't have things so rough. The idea for *Tyrell* came from my job as a social worker. I used to work with families and teenagers who were going through really hard times. Some of the teens were in gangs or used drugs and alcohol. Some of them had parents who abused or neglected them. Basically, the whole family needed help. I saw a lot of boys who were already considered to be the man of the house by their mother even though they were only fourteen or fifteen years old. So I wrote *Tyrell* because I wanted to imagine what it would be like to be fifteen years old and responsible for providing for your mother and little brother. Especially when you still had your own personal problems to deal with. I wanted to see what a typical boy would do if he had all that pressure on him and had only himself to count on.

Is there a character you would like to write more about? Does Tyrell's girlfriend get her own book?
Well, I'm planning to write a sequel to *Tyrell* as soon as I'm finished writing my second novel, *Kendra*. I'm not sure what's going to happen in the next Tyrell book, but I do know his father will be released from prison, so we will finally get to meet his "pops." I'm not sure about writing a Novisha book or a Jasmine book. Right now I don't have any ideas for what their own books would be about, but you never know!

Why did you make virginity such a big deal for Tyrell and his girlfriend? Instead of sex, could it have been drugs or something?
I never really planned to make virginity a big issue in this book; it just kind of happened on its own. I guess by having Novisha decide not to have sex with Tyrell, it showed that he respected her and really wanted to be with her, even if it meant waiting until she was ready. And I wanted to show that there are different kinds of girls in his life and each one is a challenge for him!

Did you try writing *Tyrell* without the slang and cursing? Do you think it would have been as good a book?
I didn't really think about the language before I started writing *Tyrell*. I just wanted to write about a guy, and my goal was for him to be as "real" as possible. I was kind of surprised when I wrote the first sentence and he cursed because I don't curse at all. But it seemed to be part of his personality, so I went with it. As for the slang, again, it just seemed like it was natural for him to speak that way. I didn't want to change him because then he wouldn't sound authentic. Actually, I wanted each character to have his or her own unique way of speaking.

I think it's possible to write a good book without slang and cursing, of course, but if Tyrell didn't speak that way he would have been an entirely different person. The way he speaks reflects how he was raised, where he grew up, and how he feels about everything. And it's just who he is!

Tyrell is published by Push, an imprint of Scholastic Inc.

Visit Coe Booth online: www.coebooth.com

Sitomer, Alan Lawrence
Hip-Hop High School
Jump at the Sun
Theresa and Devon,
fighting their way out
of a gang zone

Stork, Francisco X.
Behind the Eyes
Dutton
Hector, looking to avenge
his sister's death

van Diepen, Allison
Street Pharm
Simon Pulse
Brooklyn teen takes over
the family business

Volponi, Paul
Rooftop
Viking
Witness to a murder,
sent to rehab

Whittenberg, Allison
Sweet Thang
Delacorte
Charmaine, obsessed
with justice, learning
to love herself

Who Dunnit?

Abrahams, Peter
Behind the Curtain
Laura Geringer
Ingrid, locked in a car
trunk

Adams, Jane A.
Killing a Stranger
Severn House
Searching for a father's
identity can be fatal

Allison, Jennifer
Gilda Joyce
Sleuth/Dutton
Death on the grounds
of Our Lady of Sorrows

Broach, Elise
Desert Crossing
Henry Holt
3 teens and a dead body
in the road

Brockmeier, Kevin
Grooves
Katherine Tegen
Secret messages in blue
jeans and potato chips

Brooks, Kevin
The Road of the Dead
The Chicken House
Ruben and Cole: search-
ing for their sister's body

Cabot, Meg
Size 12 Is Not Fat
Avon Trade
Murder in a NYC dorm

Clements, Andrew
Things Hoped for
Philomel
Gwen's upcoming violin
audition, a missing
grandfather

Doyle, Arthur Conan,
Sir with illustrations
by Pam Smy
The Hound of the
Baskervilles
Candlewick
A classic tale revisited

Feinstein, John
Vanishing Act
Knopf
Searching for a missing
tennis player at the
U.S. Open

Ferguson, Alane
The Christopher Killer
Sleuth/Viking
Cameryn, coroner's
assistant and detective

Fforde, Jasper
The Fourth Bear
Viking
Detective Jack Spratt
searching for Goldilocks

Flynn, Gillian
Sharp Objects
Shaye Areheart
Camille, haunted by
childhood tragedy

Giles, Gail
What Happened to Cass
McBride?
Little, Brown
Kidnapped and buried
alive

Greene, Michele
Domínguez
Chasing the Jaguar
HarperCollins
Martika, Mayan heritage
and psychic powers

Haber, Melissa Glenn
The Pluto Project
Dutton
Alan, puzzles, poetry and
spying

Hartinger, Brent
Grand & Humble
HarperTempest
Harlan, Manny and an
intersection of life

Hautman, Pete and
Mary Logue
Snatched
Sleuth/Putnam
Roni and Brian solving
a kidnapping

Henry, April
Shock Point
Putnam's
Cassie, abducted and
shipped off to rehab

Jaffe, Michele
Bad Kitty
HarperCollins
Las Vegas family vacation
turns criminal

Madison, Bennett
Lulu Dark and the
Summer of the Fox
Sleuth/Razorbill
Riding a Vespa, searching
for missing actresses

Moriarty, Jaclyn
The Murder of Bindy
Mackenzie
Arthur A. Levine
Somebody really didn't
like her

Plum-Ucci, Carol
The Night My Sister Went
Missing
Harcourt
A party, a pier, a gunshot

Reiss, Kathryn
Blackthorn Winter
Harcourt
Juliana, a California girl
solving an English murder

Richards, Justin
Ghost Soldiers
Sleuth/Philomel
Solving a 1936 crime
today

Simmons, Alex and Bill,
McCay
The Raven League
Sleuth/Razorbill
Archie and friends
searching for Sherlock
Holmes

Simmons, Michael
The Rise of Lubchenko
Razorbill
Searching for the small
pox virus on the French
Riviera

Sorrells, Walter
The Silent Room
Dutton
A wicked step-father,
drugs and a Georgia
swamp

Springer, Nancy
The Case of the Missing
Marquess
Sleuth/Philomel
Enola, Sherlock's sister,
searching for her mother

Stenhouse, Ted
Murder on the Ridge
Kids Can
Wil and Arthur, solving
a 1917 murder in 1952

Stewart, Sean and Jordan
Weisman
Cathy's Book
Running Press
Dumped by Victor and
angry

Updale, Eleanor
Montmorency and the
Assassins
Orchard
International intrigue
instead of a vacation

The A-List:
Adult Novels
for Teens

Abani, Chris
Becoming Abigail
Akashic Books
Nigerian girl facing fear
in London

Berg, Elizabeth
We Are All Welcome Here
Random House
Mother/daughter
struggle for freedom

Bird, Sarah
The Flamenco Academy
Knopf
Hot love triangle with
a Spanish beat

Brewer, Sonny
A Sound Like Thunder
Ballantine
Rove's stormy 16th
summer

Carey, Lisa
Every Visible Thing
William Morrow
Emotional effects of
a missing brother

Childress, Mark
One Mississippi
Little, Brown
Best friends on prom
night gone wrong

Coupland, Douglas
JPod
Bloomsbury
A lethal joyride through
video game land

Daswani, Kavita
Salaam, Paris
Plume
A glamorous life at odds
with tradition

Furey, Leo
The Long Run
Trumpeter
A grim orphanage
enlivened by anarchy

Goodman, Allegra
Intuition
Dial
Intrigue at a cancer
research lab

Guène, Faïza
Kiffe Kiffe Tomorrow
Harvest
A Muslim girl's life in
the Parisian projects

Haulsey, Kuwana
Angel of Harlem
One World
Saving lives, breaking
barriers

Hazelwood, Robin
Model Student
Crown
College vs. the high
fashion life

Hyde, Catherine Ryan
Love in the Present Tense
Doubleday/Flying Dolphin
An abandoned child's
new beginning

Hyland, M. J.
Carry Me Down
Canongate
Detecting lies in a
cruel world

Kerney, Kelly
Born Again
Harvest
A Jesus freak's family
secrets

Kring, Sandra
The Book of Bright Ideas
Delta
New friends, big changes

Kuhlman, Evan
Wolf Boy
Shaye Areheart
Superhero's birth after
a brother dies

Lansens, Lori
The Girls
Little, Brown
Rose & Ruby: the world
of conjoined twins

McCafferty, Megan
Charmed Thirds
Crown
Jessica Darling at
Columbia University

McGovern, Cammie
Eye Contact
Viking
An autistic boy, witness
to murder

Min, Katherine
Secondhand World
Knopf
Isa, at odds with her
Korean parents

Mitchard, Jacquelyn
Cage of Stars
Warner
Murder, forgiveness,
revenge

O'Brien, Maureen
B-mother
Harcourt
The heartbreak of giving
away a baby

Pedersen, Laura
The Big Shuffle
Ballantine
Dealing with siblings
after dad dies

Pessl, Marisha
**Special Topics in
Calamity Physics**
Viking
Mysterious events for
brainiac Blue

Peterfreund, Diana
Secret Society Girl
Delacorte
Amy's Ivy League
college life

Picoult, Jodi
The Tenth Circle
Atria
Devastating truths about
Trixie's parents

Rash, Ron
The World Made Straight
Henry Holt
Travis' violent quest for
independence

Reynolds, Sheri
Firefly Cloak
Shaye Areheart
A damaged family's
attempt at love

Setterfield, Diane
The Thirteenth Tale
Atria
Learning the truth from a
famous author

Shawver, Brian
Aftermath
Nan A. Talese
Reasons behind a blue-
collar rumble

Sheehan, Aurelie
History Lesson for Girls
Viking
Friendship filled with
dreams and darkness

Sittenfeld, Curtis
The Man of My Dreams
Random House
Hannah, figuring out
what she wants

Solomon, Asali
Get Down
Farrar, Straus & Giroux
Stories of black youth,
longing to belong

Wood, Monica
Any Bitter Thing
Ballantine
Unexpected discoveries
about Lizzy's past

Woodrell, Daniel
Winter's Bone
Little, Brown
Ree's quest to find her
father

Back in
the Day

Anderson, M. T.
**The Astonishing Life
of Octavian Nothing:
Traitor to the Nation**
Candlewick
18th century ideas, an
enslaved boy, science
gone awry

Book Excerpt:
It boots us nothing to feel
rage for things that long
ago transpired. We must
curb our fury, and allow
sadness to diminish, and
speak our stories with
coolness and delibera-
tion. "Animum rege, qui
nisi paret, imperat,"
quoth the poet Horace.
"Rule thy passion, for
unless it obeys, it rules
you." I ask the Lord God
Jehovah for strength to
forgive. Whatever I have
felt about those men, I
have much to thank them
for. They lavished luxuries
upon me. They supported
my every interest and
encouraged my curiosity.
They instructed me in the
Christian religion. They
taught me the tongues of
the Greeks and the
Romans and opened for
me the colonnaded vistas
of those long-forgotten
empires, in this, the
dawning of a new empire.
They schooled me in
music, which is my
greatest delight. These
are not little things.

I do not believe they ever
meant unkindness.

Bennett, Veronica
Angelmonster
Candlewick
Mary's scandalous life
with poet Percy Shelley

Bloor, Edward
London Calling
Knopf
Martin: traveling back
in time to WWII

Collison, Linda
Star-Crossed
Knopf
Barbados-bound
stowaway becomes
surgeon's mate

Cushman, Karen
**The Loud Silence
of Francine Green**
Clarion
1950, living in the
shadow of the Cold War

Dines, Carol
Queen's Soprano
Harcourt
Forbidden to sing, 17th
century Italy

Dowswell, Paul
Prison Ship
Bloomsbury
Exiled to Australia,
Sam rethinks his future

Elyot, Amanda
**The Memoirs of Helen
of Troy**
Three Rivers
Woman abducted-the
Trojan War ignited

Ernst, Kathleen
Hearts of Stone
Dutton
Hannah's world torn apart
by the Civil War

Fletcher, Susan
Alphabet of Dreams
Atheneum
On the road to Bethle-
hem, a brother's dream,
a prophecy fulfilled

Giff, Patricia Reilly
Water Street
Wendy Lamb
1875, Bird and Thomas
living in the shadow
of the Brooklyn Bridge

Grey, Christopher
Leonardo's Shadow
Atheneum
Giacomo, becoming
a master painter

Hale, Marian
Dark Water Rising
Henry Holt
Moving to Galveston,
surviving the storm
of 1900

Hamamura, John
Color of the Sea
St. Martin's
Finding love, caught
between cultures

Hausman, Gerald and
Loretta Hausman
A Mind with Wings
Trumpeter
Henry David Thoreau,
son, brother, unrequited
lover

Hoffman, Alice
Incantation
Little, Brown
15th century Spain,
Jewish heritage, a family
betrayed

Hooper, Mary
**The Remarkable Life
and Times of Eliza Rose**
Bloomsbury
Intrigue in the London
court of Charles II

Hopkinson, Deborah
Into the Firestorm
Knopf
San Francisco, 1906, the
day the earth shook

Kadohata, Cynthia
Weedflower
Atheneum
Sumiko, exiled to
an Indian reservation
during WWII

Kerr, M. E.
Your Eyes in Stars
HarperCollins
2 friends, a prison,
a bugle player, WWII

Kidd, Ronald
Monkey Town
Simon & Schuster
The evolution of the 1925
Scopes trial

Killgore, James
The Passage
Peachtree
The Civil War, viewed from
an ironclad gun boat

Krisher, Trudy
Fallout
Holiday House
1950s: stirring up
controversy in a Southern
beach town

Larson, Kirby
Hattie Big Sky
Random House
1918, an orphan girl,
pioneer Montana farmer

Lavender, William
Aftershocks
Harcourt
1906, a family secret
revealed, San Francisco
crumbles

Lisle, Janet Taylor
Black Duck
Sleuth/Philomel
Smuggling rum during
the 1929 Prohibition

Meyer, Carolyn
Loving Will Shakespeare
Harcourt
Finding affection and
family with a young writer

Napoli, Donna Jo
Fire in the Hills
Dutton
Roberto, escaping a
Nazi labor camp, joining
the resistance

Nolan, Han
A Summer of Kings
Harcourt
A black teen accused of
a 1963 Alabama murder

Noonan, Brandon
Plenty Porter
Amulet
Living the sharecropper's
life in 1950's Illinois

Paterson, Katherine
Bread and Roses, Too
Clarion
1912, when working
conditions force a strike

Paulsen, Gary
**The Legend of Bass
Reeves**
Wendy Lamb
Former slave, larger-than-
life lawman

Pausewang, Gudrun
Dark Hours
Annick
A family survives, trapped
in a bomb shelter

Pausewang, Gudrun
Traitor
Carolrhoda Books
Anna, hiding a Russian
prisoner in Nazi Germany

Peck, Richard
Here Lies the Librarian
Dial
1914, when sorority
sisters rode into town

Salisbury, Graham
House of the Red Fish
Wendy Lamb
Tomi's family after the
Pearl Harbor attack

Whelan, Gloria
Summer of the War
HarperCollins
Belle and Carrie, whose
lives are changed in 1942

Whelan, Gloria
The Turning
HarperCollins
Tatiana dancing an
escape from the Soviet
Union

Sci Fi

Gideon, Melanie
Pucker
Razorbill
Thomas, hiding his alien
origin

Haarsma, PJ
**The Software: The Virus
on Orbis I**
Candlewick
JT, controlling computers
with his mind

Hautman, Pete
Rash
Simon & Schuster
A U.S.A. that would rather
be safe than free

Klass, David
Firestorm
Frances Foster
Jack, saving the future
from the present

Lewis, Ann Margaret
and Helen Keier
with illustrations by
Chris Trevas and
William O'Connor
**Star Wars:
The New Essential Guide
to Alien Species**
Del Rey
From the movies, novels,
comics, cartoons

Pfeffer, Susan Beth
Life as We Knew It
Harcourt
The moon's orbit
changes, everything
changes

Pow, Tom
The Pack
Roaring Brook
To rescue Floris, they
will risk it all

Stahler, David
Doppelganger
EOS
Chris Parker: Football
hero or monster?

Turtledove, Harry
In High Places
TOR
Time Trader's daughter
sold into slavery

Tutledove, Harry
**The Disunited States
of America**
TOR
War breaks out, Time
Traders are trapped

Voake, Steve
The Dreamwalker's Child
Bloomsbury
Waking in one world to
save another

Wallace, Daniel with illustrations by Ian Fullwood
Star Wars: The New Essential Guide to Droids
Del Rey
Technology from a galaxy far, far away

Fairies, Gnomes, Elves, Deities, Oh My...

Abouzeid, Chris
Anatopsis
Dutton
A princess in training to save her world

Augarde, Steve
Celandine
David Fickling
Magical fairyland in an English wood, 1915

Berryhill, Shane
Chance Fortune and the Outlaws
Starscape
Superhero dreams minus superpowers

Buckley-Archer, Linda
Gideon the Cutpurse
Simon & Schuster
Modern teens stuck in 18th century London

Carey, Janet Lee
The Beast of Noor
Atheneum
Beware the sharpness of his teeth

Connolly, John
The Book of Lost Things
Atria
Escaping grief, entering an imaginary land

Cornish, D. M.
Monster Blood Tattoo: Foundling
Putnam's
Meeting evil in many forms

Elliott, Patricia
Murkmere
Little, Brown
Challenging the belief in divine birds

Friesner, Esther
Temping Fate
Dutton
A summer job, reporting to a goddess

Gemmell, David
Troy
Del Rey
God and goddesses: at war, in love

Hale, Shannon
River Secrets
Bloomsbury
Spying in enemy territory

James, Betsy
Listening At The Gate
Atheneum
War between clans where the world began

Klause, Annette Curtis
Freaks
Margaret K. McElderry
Human oddities and an Egyptian mummy

Knox, Elizabeth
Dreamhunter
Frances Foster
Entering a place where nightmares lurk

Kushner, Ellen
The Privilege of the Sword
Bantam
Aristocratic battles in a maze of secrets

Langrish, Katherine
Troll Mill
EOS
Protecting a seal-woman's baby

Larbalestier, Justine
Magic Lessons
Razorbill
In Australia, unlocking secret knowledge

Le Guin, Ursula K.
Voices
Harcourt
Memer, heir to secrets preserved in books

Leavitt, Martine
Keturah and Lord Death
Front Street
Telling a tale, finding her true love

Levine, Gail Carson
Fairest
HarperCollins
A magical mirror, a beautiful voice

Marcus, Leonard S., editor
Wand In the Word
Candlewick
Interviews with master storytellers

McCaffrey, Laura Williams
Water Shaper
Clarion
A princess drawn to the sea

Meyer, Kai
Pirate Curse
Margaret K. McElderry
Polliwogs' special talents to fight evil

Miller, Kirsten
Kiki Strike
Bloomsbury
Exploring the city's underground secrets

Moers, Walter
Rumo & His Miraculous Adventures
Overlook
Hero of Zamonia: a talking dog with horns

Moesta, Rebecca and Kevin J. Anderson
Crystal Doors
Little, Brown
Cousins transported to a magical island

Morpurgo, Michael, illustrated by Michael Foreman
Beowulf
Candlewick
Saving the kingdom from three evils

November, Sharyn, editor
Firebirds Rising
Firebird
Stories where fantasy takes flight

Osborne, Mary Pope
Haunted Waters
Candlewick
In love with a mysterious sea maiden

Papademetriou, Lisa
The Wizard, the Witch & Two Girls from Jersey
Razorbill
Mistaken for heroines in a fantasy story

Park, Paul
The Tourmaline
TOR
Miranda in an alternative Europe

Paver, Michelle
Spirit Walker
Katherine Tegan
When a deadly illness afflicts the clans

Pierce, Tamora
Terrier
Random House
Rookie crime fighter in a world of magic

Pratchett, Terry
Wintersmith
HarperTempest
Seasons stop for a witch
in training

Riordan, Rick
Sea of Monsters
Miramax
Percy and his friends:
demigods

Ruby, Laura
The Wall and the Wing
EOS
Flying boy, invisible girl

Just My Opinion!

*I really enjoyed the book
[The Wall and the Wing],
even the evil parts
involving Mrs. Terwilliger
and her monkeys. It has
the typical orphan in New
York story with not-so-
typical odd-ins. For example,
I found it awesome that
there were albino alligators
in the subway and that the
lions outside of the main
library were really sweaty
men in lion suits. The way
the author describes the
subway at night makes it
seem like such a dark,
unfriendly place, and I love
how she did this without
coming out and saying it.
Some parts of the book
skeeve me out, like the
sewer rats from Satan and
how they worship cats.
But on a more positive
note, I never wanted to
stop reading this book
and though I was annoyed
that the end of the book
was set up for a sequel,
I'm happy too.*
Teen Reviewer:
Emily Atlas
Jefferson Market Branch
Library, Manhattan

Russell, Karen
**St. Lucy's Home for Girls
Raised by Wolves**
Knopf
Surrealistic tales of the
Everglades

Russon, Penni
Undine
Greenwillow
Discovering her father
and her own power

Just My Opinion!

*A bittersweet, mysterious
book [Undine], this first
novel by Ms. Russon is
not something you'll put
down until you've read it
more than once. Undine,
a young Australian
teenager, becomes the
source for powerful and
dynamic magic. Who is
she? Where did she come
from? What mark will
she leave on the world?
All of these are answered
in breathtaking prose.
The beautiful symbolism
and speculations that
resonate in this book
will haunt you with their
insight.*
Teen Reviewer:
Pearl Mutnick
St. Agnes Branch Library,
Manhattan

Sage, Angie
Flyte
Katherine Tegen
Growing into wizardry

Shinn, Sharon
**The Dream Maker's
Magic**
Viking
The fate of a girl raised
as a boy

Shusterman, Neal
Everlost
Simon & Schuster
Nick & Allie caught
between life & death

Smith, Gordon
The Forest in the Hallway
Clarion
Miscast spells and
encounters with Death

Snyder, Maria V.
Magic Study
Luna
One year to harness her
power or die

Stanley, Diane
Bella At Midnight
HarperCollins
A peasant girl of noble
birth

Sutherland, Tui T.
So This Is How It Ends
EOS
Teen survivors of
earth's demise

Topsell, John
**How to Raise and Keep
a Dragon**
Barron's
Choose carefully: they
live for centuries

Turner, Megan Whalen
The King of Attolia
Greenwillow
A former thief's royal
potential

Ursu, Anne
The Shadow Thieves
Atheneum
Into the underground
world to save the earth

Valente, Catherynne M.
In the Night Garden
Bantam Spectra
Stories inked on a lonely
girl's eyelids

Weiss, M. Jerry, and Helen
S. Weiss, editors
Dreams and Visions
Starscape
Imaginative tales by
authors you know

Winterson, Jeanette
Tanglewreck
Bloomsbury
Bizarre time warps

Wooding, Chris
Storm Thief
Scholastic
Where violent tempests
alter reality

Graphic
Novels

Campbell, Eddie
The Fate of the Artist
First Second
Investigating his own
disappearance

Eldred, Tim
Grease Monkey
TOR
Robin's new boss:
an 800 pound gorilla

Fies, Brian
Mom's Cancer
Abrams Image
How a disease affects
an entire family

Gravett, Paul
Graphic Novels
Collins Design
Stories to change your life

Hernandez, Gilbert
Sloth
DC Comics
Waking up from an
unexplained coma

Jacobson, Sid
**The 9/11 Report: A
Graphic Adaptation**
Hill and Wang
A new look at the day
that changed us

Kibuishi, Kazu
Flight 3
Ballantine
Magical, mysteries, and
marvelous stories

McCloud, Scott
Making Comics
HarperCollins
Writing, lettering, inking,
creating

Myrick, Leland
Missouri Boy
First Second
Beautiful and ugly
memories of growing up

Rocks, Misako
Biker Girl
Hyperion
Racing for a family's
honor

Rollins, Prentis
**The Making of a Graphic
Novel/ The Resonator**
Watson-Guptill
The creation of The
Resonator

Sfar, Joann
Vampire Loves
First Second
Tales of romance, both
living and undead

Just My Opinion!

*Vampire Ferdinand has
trouble finding love as he
flies through the world
and dates a tree nymph,
another vampire and a
ghost. With humor,
fantasy and an interesting
insight of life, Sfar's
graphic novel is quick
and entertaining read.*
Teen Reviewer:
Norma N. Perez-
Hernandez
Kingsbridge Branch
Library, Bronx

Vaughan, Brian K.
Pride of Baghdad
Vertigo
Lions learn that freedom
has a price

Veitch, Rick
Can't Get No
DC Comics
One man, transformed
by permanent markers

Verne, Jules, adapted by
Rod Whigham
**20,000 Leagues
Under the Sea:
The Graphic Novel**
DK
A sea monster, a subma-
rine, and a secret

Weinstein, Lauren R.
Girl Stories
Henry Holt
"I am so cool" and other
tales of woe

Wood, Brian and Becky
Cloonan
Demo
AiT/Planet Lar
12 stories, teens at the
crossroads

Yang, Gene Luen
American Born Chinese
First Second
Fables, sterotypes and real life

Manga: I ♥ Japan and Other Places Too

Chmakova, Svetlana
Dramacon, Volume 2
Tokyopop
Cosplay turns to love play

Endo, Minari
Dazzle, Volume 1
Tokyopop
Man on a mission meets a magical girl

Hayashi, Fumino
Neon Genesis Evangelion, Volume 1
ADV Manga
Love instead of war

Hiromu, Mutou
Never Give Up, Volume 1
Tokyopop
Protecting the man she loves

Kobayashi, Jin
School Rumble, Volume 1
Del Rey
Bad boy vs. boring boy, hearts crumble

Kotegawa, Yua
Anne Freaks, Volume 1
ADV Manga
Murdering teens might have a reason

Mochizuki, Minetaro
Dragon Head, Volume 1
Tokyopop
3 survivors may not survive each other

Mukai, Natsumi
+Anima, Volume 1
Tokyopop
Orphans with animal powers becoming a family

Soryo, Fuyumi
ES, Volume 1
Del Rey
Hack minds, rearrange memories

Sugisaki, Yukiru
RizelMine
Tokyopop
Married at 15 to a 12-year-old superbeing

Vampires, Bats, Scaredy Cats

Almond, David
Clay
Delacorte
A new boy who brings sculpture to life

Austin, Joanne, complier
Weird Hauntings
Sterling
True tales of ghostly places

Carter, Dean Vincent
The Hand of the Devil
Delacorte
Headline: a very deadly mosquito

Duval, Alex
Bloodlust
Simon Pulse
Fashion, film and fangs in Malibu

Gantos, Jack
The Love Curse of the Rumbaughs
Farrar Straus & Giroux
Preserving memories of mommy

Book Excerpt:
Then, at the moment my heart began to race from fear, I realized I had seen that taut, determined face before. I was certain. Suddenly it came over me that she was Ab and Dolph's mother, because she looked exactly like the large sepia-toned photograph they had of her in their upstairs office. It was the same dress, and same creepy shawl, and same "secret" smile. This was all churning roughly in my mind, and I turned away as if looking in another direction might erase what I had discovered. And then some impulse jerked me back around and I looked at her again. I had to be sure of what I saw before I said anything upstairs. At that moment one of the little wheels shifted, and she abruptly tipped forward.

Holder, Nancy
Pretty Little Devils
Razorbill
Dying to be part of the in crowd

Horowitz, Anthony
Evil Star
Scholastic
Shutting the gate against demons

Horowitz, Anthony
Horowitz Horror
Philomel
Killer cameras and creepy computers

Jablonski, Carla
Thicker Than Water
Razorbill
Kia's desperate craving in her veins

Kasischke, Laura
Boy Heaven
HarperTempest
Stalking, threatening, haunting

Libby, Alisa M.
The Blood Confession
Dutton
A young noblewoman's bizarre beauty baths

Meyer, Stephenie
New Moon
Little, Brown
Star-crossed vampire love

Book Excerpt:
But this was no dream, and, unlike the nightmare, I wasn't running for my life; I was racing to save something infinitely more precious. My own life meant little to me today.

Alice had said there was a good chance we would both die here. Perhaps the outcome would be different if she weren't trapped by the brilliant sunlight; only I was free to run across this bright, crowded square.

And I couldn't run fast enough.

So it didn't matter to me that we were surrounded by our extraordinarily dangerous enemies. As the clock began to toll out the hour, vibrating under the soles of my sluggish feet, I knew I was too late—and I was glad something bloodthirsty waited in the wings. For in failing at this, I forfeited any desire to live.

The clock tolled again, and the sun beat down from the exact center point of the sky.

Rees, Douglas
The Janus Gate
Watson-Guptill
A classic painting of a mysterious family

Roman, Benjamin and Keith Griffen
I Luv Halloween, Volume 1
Tokyopop
When tricksters don't get the right treats

Saul, John
In the Dark of the Night
Ballantine
Assembling the tools of terror

Shan, Darren
Demon Thief
Little, Brown
Through a window into an evil universe

Westerfeld, Scott
The Last Days
Razorbill
Playing in a band as NYC falls apart

one world

Africa

Adichie, Chimamanda Ngozi
Half of a Yellow Sun
Knopf
A civil war erupts,
3 Nigerians run for
their lives

Glass, Linzi
The Year the Gypsies Came
Henry Holt
A family's innocence lost
during South Africa's
apartheid

Houze, David
Twilight People
University of California
From South Africa to
Mississippi and back,
one man's roots

Hunter-Gault, Charlayne
New News Out of Africa
Oxford
Examining issues of a
complex continent

Korn, Fadumo with
Sabine Eichhorst
Born in the Big Rains
The Feminist Press
Memories of Somalia
and female circumcision

O'Donnell, Beth and
Kimberly Sevcik
Angels in Africa
Vendome
Profiles of seven
extraordinary women

Rusesabagina, Paul
with Tom Zoellner
An Ordinary Man
Viking
Torn between two
Rwandan worlds: Hutu
or Tutsi

Asia

Chen, Da
Brothers
Shaye Areheart
Strangers become
enemies in 1960s China

Ellis, Deborah
Jackal in the Garden
Watson-Guptill
Encountering an artist
in 15th-century Persia

Gratz, Alan
Samurai Shortstop
Dial
Caught between new
and old Japan

Jaffrey, Madhur
Climbing the Mango Trees
Knopf
Tasty memories of
growing up in India

Kang, Hyok
This Is Paradise!
Little, Brown
Surviving childhood in
North Korea

Lat
Kampung Boy
First Second
Comic life in 1950s
Malaysia

Lewis, Richard
The Killing Sea
Simon & Schuster
Sarah's family caught
in a tsunami

McCormick, Patricia
Sold
Hyperion
From poverty to sexual
slavery in India

Book Excerpt:
Auntie is speaking to a
man in a tongue I do not
understand. Some of the
words are familiar, but
most of them rush by like
the huts-and-shops-and-
huts-and-shops, making
my head hurt from the
speed of this city talk.
    It seems as though
they are talking about me
now. The man, who has a
nose like a turnip, points
to me and asks Auntie a
question. The answer, as
best I can tell, is the
number twelve.
    He trains his eyes on
me and my pink dress,
and I imagine that he can
see right through it. I wrap
my arms around myself.
"How old are you?" he
says in my language.
I tell him I am thirteen.
    He wheels around and
slaps Auntie across the
face, and she turns from a
woman of queenly bearing
to a frightened child.
    The turnip-nose man
lets out a stream of angry
words I cannot follow, but
I understand that I have
done wrong. I fall to my
knees and beg the man to
forgive me.
    But he and Auntie are
laughing. They are
speaking in a strange
language, but it seems
that they are trading
numbers.
    Auntie names a price
as high as a mountain.
The man spits.

Sheth, Kashmira
Koyal Dark, Mango Sweet
Hyperion
Jeeta, facing an arranged
marriage

Stewart, Rory
The Places in Between
Harvest
A walk through war-torn
Afghanistan

Thompson, Sandy
One in A Billion
powerHouse
Getting to know the soul
of China

Europe

Baricco, Alessandro
An Iliad
Knopf
The siege of Troy retold

Mackall, Dandi Daley
Eva Underground
Harcourt
Helping freedom fighters
in 1970s Poland

Naidoo, Beverley
Web of Lies
Amistad
Femi, 12, forced to join
a violent London gang

Schmemann, Serge
When the Wall Came Down
Kingfisher
Eye witness to German
reunification

Wallace, Karen
The Unrivalled Spangles
Atheneum
Circus act sisters try
for better lives

Never Again: The Holocaust

Boyne, John
The Boy in the Striped Pajamas
David Fickling
Out-with/Auschwitz-
friends and a fence

Just My Opinion!
The Boy in the Striped
Pajamas *is about a nine-
year-old boy named
Bruno. He was forced to
move from his friends and
home in Berlin. This made
Bruno very sad. At his
new house he was
separated by a fence from
all. Little did he know the
people on the other side
of the fence were Jews.
His father took part in
running a concentration
camp. I, in fact, loved
the boy.*
Sashalee King
West Farms Branch
Library, Bronx

Friedman, D. Dina
Escaping into the Night
Simon & Schuster
Through underground
tunnels into a forest

Glatshteyn, Yankev
Emil and Karl
Roaring Brook
Friends surviving in
pre-war Vienna

Greif, Jean-Jacques
The Fighter
Bloomsbury
Boxing to live, surviving
death camps

Katin, Miriam
We Are On Our Own
Drawn & Quarterly
Fleeing Budapest ahead
of the Nazis

Kirschner, Ann
Sala's Gift
Free Press
My mother: 7 work
camps, 5 years

Book Excerpt:
Sal perched his hands on his hips and gazed at him dead-on, "Then what do you care if I'm gay or not?"

Carlos shifted his feet. Now that he actually stood face-to-face with Sal, the whole makeover idea seemed not only crazy, but embarrassingly stupid. Yet, given what Sal thought Carlos wanted, he felt he had to explain himself. "It's just, um, I wanted to ask if you could, um"—he cleared his throat—"help me?"

Sal gave him a long, steady look. Then his brow softened. "Look, dude," he said gently. "If you think you're gay you probably are. I can't tell you if you are or not. Join the Gay-Straight Alliance we're starting. That'll help you figure it out."

interview

Members of the Nathan Straus Teen Central's Teen Advisory Group offer questions via Email to Alex Sanchez, the author of *Getting It*.

What inspired you to write *Getting It*?
I get emails from a lot of gay teenage boys, and from lesbian, bisexual, and straight girls, but not from a lot of straight boys. When I finally heard from one, I thought, wow! How did that happen? I emailed back and asked him questions, and imagined what it would be like for a straight boy to become friends with an openly gay boy … but I couldn't come up with a story. Then the TV show *Queer Eye for the Straight Guy* started and I thought, that's my story: a queer eye for the straight TEEN BOY!

How was writing *Getting It* different from writing your other books?
I think the big difference was writing from the perspective of a straight teen boy. I hadn't done that in a novel before. Beyond that, every book presents its own challenges in terms of telling the story, understanding the characters, and capturing the voice.

When you were a teenager, did you have to face any of the struggles that any of your characters do?
Even though my books are fiction, a lot of what I write is based on my own experience. As a teen I experienced a lot of the struggles the characters in my novels go through with their families and the name-calling and put-downs they experience at school.

What do you do for inspiration when you get writer's block?
I have too many ideas to get writer's block in the sense that people usually think of it. The biggest block I have is getting the patience to sit and write and re-write. The hardest thing is making myself sit down. Once I can do that, the writing and re-writing flow.

What inspired you to write?
I think my passion comes from all the things I was afraid to say when I was a teenager. Now I am saying them.

What inspired you to think of *So Hard to Say*?
I got emails from young people in middle school, 11, 12, and 13 years old, and heard from middle school teachers and librarians that they'd like to have a book for and about students that age dealing with gay-straight issues. In terms of the story, I heard from so many teenage straight girls (and adult women) who fell in love with a guy who turned out to be gay.

Within the Rainbow series and *So Hard to Say*, what characters can you relate to most?
All of them. The way I breathe life into a character is by identifying how I am like him or her and how they are like me.

Have you written (or would you write) any lesbian books?
Not yet. I've written lesbian characters, but not a whole book. Maybe some day.

Getting It is published by Simon & Schuster Books for Young Readers. Visit Alex Sanchez online: www.alexsanchez.com

Jaramillo, Ann
La Línea
Roaring Brook
Miguel and Elena,
crossing the Mexican
border to the USA

Nazario, Sonia
Enrique's Journey
Random House
A Hondouran boy's search
to find his mother

Ostow, Micol
**Emily Goldberg Learns
to Salsa**
Razorbill
A Jewish girl discovers
her Puerto Rican roots

Resau, Laura
What the Moon Saw
Delacorte
Grandparents and magic
in Yucoyoo, Mexico

Sanchez, Alex
Getting It
Simon & Schuster
Carlos and Sal–each
needing a favor

Serros, Michele
Honey Blonde Chica
Simon Pulse
Evie: Flojo chick or
sophisticated Sangro

Native Americans

Bruchac, Joseph
Wabi
Dial
A hero owl in love with
a human girl

Crow, Joseph Medicine
Counting Coup
National Geographic
What it means to be a
tribal chief

Hungrywolf, Adolf
The Tipi
Native Voices
History of the traditional
dwelling

Kudlinski, Kathleen V.
My Lady, Pocahontas
Marshall Cavendish
Neetah, her friend, tells
the story

Smelcer, John
The Trap
Henry Holt
Albert, staying alive until
help arrives

U.S.A Black Voices, Black Experiences

Draper, Sharon M.
Copper Sun
Atheneum
Amari, fleeing to Fort
Mose, escaping slavery

Fradin, Judith Bloom and
Dennis Brindell Fradin
5,000 Miles to Freedom
National Geographic
A couple disguised,
fleeing slavery

Freedman, Russell
Freedom Walkers
Holiday House
The boycotting beginning
segregation's end

Helfer, Andrew with
art by Randy DuBurke
**Malcolm X:
A Graphic Biography**
*Hill and Wang/Serious
Comics*
Portrait of a charismatic
leader

Landau, Elaine
**Fleeing to Freedom
on the Underground
Railroad**
21st Century
Documenting a network
of courage

Lester, Julius
Time's Memory
Farrar, Straus & Giroux
Ekundayo, finding peace
for the spirits of dead
slaves

Myers, Walter Dean
The Harlem Hellfighters
Amistad/HarperCollins
Fighting for the United
States in WWI

Rampersad, Arnold and
David Roessel, editors
with illustrations by
Benny Andrews
Langston Hughes
Sterling
African American life in
rhythmic verse

Siegelson, Kim L.
Honey Bea
Jump at the Sun
Slave girl, discovers the
secrets of the past

U.S.A. Past and Present

Bausum, Ann
Freedom Riders
National Geographic
Traveling by bus to end
segregation

Cooper, Michael L.
Hero of the High Seas
National Geographic
John Paul Jones, swash-
buckling risk-taker

Doak, Robin with Robert
Olwell
Georgia
National Geographic
1521-1776: A colony for
those in need of a second
chance

Gillon, Steven M.
**Ten Days That
Unexpectedly
Changed America**
Three Rivers
May 16, 1637-June 21,
1964: Dates from our
national memory

Hopkinson, Deborah
Up Before Daybreak
Scholastic Nonfiction
King Cotton: sucking the
life blood of workers

Jarrow, Gail
The Printer's Trial
Calkins Creek
Peter Zenger and the
struggle for a free press

Lefkowitz, Arthur S.
Bushnell's Submarine
Scholastic Nonfiction
Attempting to sink a
British warship in NY
harbor

Oppenheim, Joanne
Dear Miss Breed
Scholastic Nonfiction
Voices from the Japanese
American internment
camps

Ritchie, Donald A. and
JusticeLearning.org
Our Constitution
Oxford
Not perfect, but neces-
sary for our freedom

Slatta, Richard W.
Cowboy
Sterling
Riding the range on
horseback

Van den Bogaert and
George O'Connor
**Journey into Mohawk
Country**
First Second
A long-dead Dutch
trader's journal in
pictures

Wheeler, Tom
Mr. Lincoln's T-Mails
Collins
Using the telegraph to
win the Civil War

Zeitz, Joshua
Flapper
Crown
Modern women of the
1920s

New York, NY

Arbus, Amy with an essay
by A.M. Homes
On the Street:1980-1990
Welcome
Nonconformity, style,
charisma, pure 80s,
pure fun

Gethard, Chris
Weird New York
Sterling
The bizarre, the odd,
the ghostly...for real

Martinez, Hugo
Graffiti NYC
Prestel
Buildings, billboards,
rooftops, subway cars

Schlesinger, Toni
**Five flights Up
and Other New York
Apartment Stories**
Princeton Architectural
Life inside NYC homes
revealed

Taylor, Kim
Bowery Girl
Viking
1883: Lower East
Side, pickpockets
and prostitutes

right here right now

Dealing With It

Antieau, Kim
Mercy, Unbound
Simon Pulse
The dangerous delusions of an anorexic

Bornstein, Kate
Hello Cruel World
Seven Stories
Survival guide for freaky outsiders

Brenna, Beverley
Wild Orchid
Red Deer
Taylor, pushing the limits of her autism

Corman, Catherine A. and Edward M. Hollowell
Positively ADD
Walker
Successful lives despite this syndrome

Garrison, Julia Fox
Don't Leave Me This Way
HarperCollins
A sudden stroke, a life altered

Johnson, Harriet McBride
Accidents of Nature
Henry Holt
Self-image adjustment at disability camp

Knighton, Ryan
Cockeyed
Public Affairs
Descent into blindness at age 18

Koss, Amy Goldman
Side Effects
Roaring Brook
Izzy's defiant bout with lymphoma

Nelson, Richard E. and Judith C. Galos
The Power to Prevent Suicide
Free Spirit
The tools to help someone you know

Nuzum, K. A.
A Small White Scar
Joanna Cotler
His disabled twin's role in Will's future

Just My Opinion!

The story, A Small White Scar, *describes two brothers that are rodeo horse players and how they worked together. It describes how people challenged themselves to become better. The brothers have their ups and downs and one brother becomes scared about riding a horse again. Why? Because he becomes hurt and realizes that he could do something better. These two brothers were supposed to be blood brothers forever. Then everything all changes.*
Teen Reviewer: Antonio Martinez West Farms Branch Library, Bronx

Rorby, Ginny
Hurt Go Happy
Starscape
The chimp that taught Joey sign language

Schutz, Samantha
I Don't Want to Be Crazy
PUSH
A girl's struggle with anxiety disorder

Scowen, Kate
My Kind of Sad
Annick
What it's like to be young and depressed

Serotte, Brenda
The Fortune Teller's Kiss
Univ. of Nebraska Pr.
A Bronx youth: A Sephardic Jew with polio

Turner, Ann Warren
Hard Hit
Scholastic
Mark's great life, except his dad dies

Vaught, Susan
Trigger
Bloomsbury
Life after a gunshot to the head

Zupan, Mark
Gimp
HarperCollins
Amazing life of a quadriplegic athlete

Book Excerpt (*Gimp*):
There's a quote by distance runner, philosopher, and author George Sheehan that explains how I feel about athletics and why I love to play:

Sport is where an entire life can be compressed into a few hours, where the emotions of a lifetime can be felt on an acre or two of ground, where a person can suffer and die and rise again on six miles of trails through a New York City park. Sport is a theater where the sinner can turn saint and a common man become an uncommon hero, where the past and future can fuse with the present. Sport is singularly able to give us peak experiences where we feel completely one with the world and transcend all conflicts as we fully become our own potential.

Traumatic injury can have a similar effect. It's a giant lens that makes you refocus your life. It's an X-ray for the guts and soul, the ultimate bullshit test. It forces you to inspect what you're truly made of, past the fatty lasers of self-deceit and denial, clear down to the bone and marrow of your true being. Break your neck and you'll quickly get to know yourself. Intimately. You'll learn who your true friends are. You'll figure out what family really means.

Do You Believe?

Allen, Judy
Unexplained
Kingfisher
Puzzles science hasn't solved

Boughn, Michael
Into the World of the Dead
Annick
Monsters, demons, heroes in the Underworld

Chopra, Deepak
Teens Ask Deepak
Simon Pulse
Questions and answers about spirituality

Garfinkel, Perry
Buddha or Bust
Harmony
Global journey to enlightenment

Kumar, Satish
The Buddha and the Terrorist
Algonquin
Turning evil to good

Strelecky, John P.
The Why Café
Da Capo
Diner at the crossroads of your life

Getting It Together

Boutaudou, Sylvie
Weighing In
Amulet
Conquering body issues

DeVillers, Julia
The College Dorm Survival Guide
Three Rivers
Everything you need to know

Fedorko, Jamie
The Intern Files
Simon Spotlight Entertainment
Getting a rung up on your career ladder

Fletcher, Anne M.
Weight Loss Confidential
Houghton Mifflin
Successful strategies
for teens

Harper, Hill
**Letters to a Young
Brother**
Gotham
Straight talk about
school, work, girls...

Harrison, Blake and
Alexander Rappaport
Flocabulary
Cider Mill
Soundtrack to your
SAT success

Haskins-Booker, Laura
Dreams to Reality
Morning Glory
Helping teen moms
achieve success

Jacobs, Tom
**What Are My Rights?
updated edition**
Free Spirit
Questions and answers
for teens

Levy, Barrie
In Love and In Danger
Seal
Getting out of abusive
relationships

Sewell, Michelle, editor
Growing Up Girl
GirlChild
Life-changing moments
in poetry and prose

Toronto Public Library
Research Virtuoso
Annick
Seeking, sourcing and
sorting information

Walsh, Marissa, editor
**Not Like I'm Jealous
or Anything**
Delacorte
Understanding the
green-eyed monster

True Crime & Justice

Fletcher, Connie
**Every Contact Leaves
a Trace**
St. Martin's
The real world, not CSI

Parker, Derrick with
Matt Diehl
Notorious C.O.P.
St. Martin's
Working in the NYPD Rap
Intelligence Unit

Rainis, Kenneth G.
Blood and DNA Evidence
Enslow
Crime-solving science
experiments

Souter, Gerry
**Secret Service Agent and
Careers in Federal
Protection**
Enslow
Risking your life for your
country

Wagner, E. J.
**The Science of
Sherlock Holmes**
Wiley
Fact, fiction and the
history of forensics

LGBTQ

Bechdel, Alison
Fun Home
Houghton Mifflin
Trapped in the family-
owned funeral home

Jennings, Kevin
**Mama's Boy,
Preacher's Son**
Beacon
A leader's rise from
poverty, racism and
homophobia

Levithan, David
Wide Awake
Knopf
Duncan & Co.: racing
to save the first gay,
Jewish president

Levithan, David and
Billy Merrell, editors
The Full Spectrum
Knopf
Real queer life captured
in poetry, prose, letters,
photography

O'Neal, Hank
Gay Day
Abrams Image
Balloons, banners,
buttons: The big NYC
Pride Parade

Peters, Julie Anne
Between Mom and Jo
Megan Tingley
Nick: stuck in the
middle of his mother
and her wife

Sloan, Brian
Tale of Two Summers
Simon & Schuster
Hal and Chuck's madcap
summer apart

Spanbauer, Tom
Now Is the Hour
Houghton Mifflin
Rigby John, thumbing his
way from Idaho to San
Francisco

Tewksbury, Mark
Inside Out
Wiley
A swimmer's journey
out of the closet and
into Olympic gold

Tuaolo, Esera with
John Rosengren
Alone in the Trenches
Sourcebooks
An NFL player's secret life

Looking Good

Gay, Kathlyn
Am I Fat?
Enslow
Obesity, teens and
what to do about it

Schlip, Joanna
Glamour Gurlz
Clarkson Potter
From ordinary
to extraordinary

Walsh, Marissa
Girl With Glasses
Simon Spotlight
Living life with four eyes

Weingarten, Rachel C.
Hello Gorgeous!
Collectors Press
Looking back at beauty
products

Memoirs: All About Moi

Baskin, Julia,
Lindsey Newman,
Sophie Pollitt-Cohen
and Courtney Toombs
The Notebook Girls
Warner
The diary of 4 Stuyvesant
H.S. girls gone wild

Blackwell, Unita with
JoAnne Prichard Morris
Barefootin'
Crown
From sharecropper to
White House confidante

Caldwell, Gail
A Strong West Wind
Random House
Memories of family
in Texas

Cooper, Anderson
Dispatches from the Edge
HarperCollins
The search for truths in
a topsy-turvy world

Dornstein, Ken
**The Boy Who Fell Out
of the Sky**
Random House
A brother's life revealed
following a plane crash

Dunn, Jancee
But Enough About Me
HarperCollins
Backstage and behind the
scenes with celebrities

Eisenstein, Bernice
**I Was a Child of
Holocaust Survivors**
Riverhead
Escaping Auschwitz
but reliving its horrors

Erlbaum, Janice
Girlbomb
Villard
On the streets of NYC,
a life chaotic

Franzen, Jonathan
The Discomfort Zone
Farrar Straus & Giroux
Author, birdwatcher,
prankster

Miró, Asha
Daughter of the Ganges
Atria
Divided between being
Indian and Spanish

Nissel, Angela
Mixed
Villard
Crossing the lines
of black and white

Mind, Body, Love, Sex

Brynie, Faith Hickman
**101 Questions About
Sleep and Dreams**
21st Century
Answers about your
body's down time

Firlik, Katrina
**Another Day in the
Frontal Lobe**
Random House
Sometimes it is brain
surgery

Goldsmith, Connie
Invisible Invaders
21st Century
Infectious diseases,
a world-wide problem

Grady, Denise
Deadly Invaders
Kingfisher
Virus outbreaks
around the world

Hager, Thomas
**Demon Under the
Microscope**
Harmony
Finding the first
miracle drug

Hyde, Margaret O and Elizabeth H. Forsyth
Safe Sex 101
21st Century
Prevent disease, pregnancy and heartache

Hyman, Bruce M. and Cherry Pedrick
Anxiety Disorders
21st Century
Recognize when help is needed

Luadzers, Darcy
Virgin Sex for Girls
Hatherleigh
Real stories about first experiences

Luadzers, Darcy
Virgin Sex for Guys
Hatherleigh
Having safe and healthy relationships

Moffett, Shannon
The Three-Pound Enigma
Workman
Understanding the brain

Silverstein, Alvin, Virginia Silverstein and Laura Silverstein Nunn
The STDs Update
Enslow
The facts that can protect you

St. Stephen's Community House
The Little Black Book for Girlz
Annick
Frank advice from Toronto teens

The Editors of CosmoGIRL!
Ask CosmoGIRL! About Guys
Hearst
Dealing with dating dilemmas

The Editors of CosmoGIRL!
Ask CosmoGIRL! About Your Body
Hearst
Intimate questions, honest answers

Weschler, Toni
Cycle Savvy
Collins
Girls' guide to her monthly period

Superstars, Heroes, Everyday People

Abrahamson, Jennifer
Sweet Relief
Simon Spotlight Entertainment
Protester, partygirl, advocate for peace

Clash, Kevin with Gary Brozek
My Life As a Furry Red Monster
Broadway
The man behind Elmo

Book Excerpt:
When I tell folks what I do for a living ("What'dya mean you're Elmo? You're a forty-five-year-old six-foot African American male with a deep voice, get outta here"), after they regain their composure, they ask me to explain Elmo's popularity. Elmo is instantly recognizable in nearly every country in the world. He knows heads of state, A-list celebrities, world-class athletes, Oscar winners, Tony winners, Grammy winners, spelling-bee winners, and lots of babies. If Elmo had a cell phone, it would never stop ringing. Why is this little fur-and-foam bundle of energy such a phenomenon?

I have a one-word answer: love. Elmo connects with children and adults on the purest and most fundamental level, and that is the human desire to love and be loved. It's as simple as that.

Colman, Penny
Adventurous Women
Henry Holt
Reporter, explorers, super sleuths, fierce fighters

Dunn, Brad
When They Were 22
Andrews McMeel
Celebrity oops, goofs, transformations

Gelletly, LeeAnne
Gift of Imagination
Morgan Reynolds
Roald Dahl: author, illustrator, prankster

Hoobler, Dorothy and Thomas Hoobler
The Monsters
Little, Brown
Free love and scandal, Mary Shelley and her circle

Jennings, Ken
Brainiac
Villard
Trivia's undisputed king

Kimmel, Elizabeth Cody
Ladies First
National Geographic
Notable women, intimate portraits

Konstam, Angus
Blackbeard
Wiley
A ruthless, cutthroat, pirate

Krull, Kathleen
Sigmund Freud
Viking
Earning his cred with the human head

Mainardi, Alessandro, Werner Maresta, and Federico Pietrobon
The Life of Pope John Paul II...in Comics!
Papercutz
A leader's rise to the papacy

McClafferty, Carla Killough
Something Out Of Nothing
Farrar Straus & Giroux
Marie Curie: science, discovery, life

McDermott, Keith J.
Lessons From Our Fathers
Durban House
How dads' wisdom shaped their lives

Naden, Corinne J.
Fidel Castro and the Cuban Revolution
Morgan Reynolds
A portrait of a nation's leader

Reef, Catherine
E. E. Cummings
Clarion
The poet who bent and broke rules

Scott, Christina
Nelson Mandela
Gramercy
From Troublemaker to Nobel Laureate

Shalit, Willa, editor
Becoming Myself
Hyperion
Girls growing up, learning to love

Shields, Charles J.
Mockingbird
Henry Holt
Harper Lee: unconventional, high-spirited, hardheaded

Smiley, Tavis
What I Know for Sure
Doubleday
From trailer park to talk show stardom

Spragins, Ellyn, editor
What I Know Now
Broadway
Letters from 40 women to their younger selves

That's Hot

Atkin, S. Beth
Gunstories
Katherine Tegen
For good or ill, life-changing forces

Fulbeck, Kip
Part Asian, 100% Hapa
Chronicle
Portraits of people of mixed race

Goldman, Paula, editor
Imagining Ourselves
New World
Global voices, a new generation of women

Guitton, Pedro
T-Shirt 360º
Gingko
612 weird, witty, ironic, iconic designs

Haenfler, Ross
Straight Edge
Rutgers Univ.
Being cool, minus alcohol, drugs and sex

Husain, Sarah, editor
Voices of Resistance
Seal
Muslim women in a post 9/11 world

Montague, Julian
The Stray Shopping Carts of Eastern North America
Abrams Image
Four-wheeled clutter in our environment

Reichblum, Charles
What Happens to a Torn Dollar Bill?
Black Dog & Leventhal
Everything you want to know about money

Roberts, David and Jeremy Leslie
Pick Me Up
DK
Factoids everyone should know

Rothbart, Davy, editor
Found II
Fireside
Lost notes, pictures, even shopping lists

Schlosser, Eric and
Charles Wilson
Chew on This
Houghton Mifflin
And never eat fast
food again

Sullivan, James
Jeans
Gotham
Denim: from work
clothing to high fashion

War and Peace

Axe, David and
Steven Olexa
War Fix
NBM/ComicsLit
A graphic novel of the
frontlines in Iraq

Buell, Hal
**Uncommon Valor,
Common Virtue**
Berkley Calilber
Raising the flag at
Iwo Jima

Carroll, Andrew, editor
Operation Homecoming
Random House
Iraq and Afghanistan in
the words of U.S troops
and their families

Coleman, Janet Wyman
with the International
Spy Museum
**Secrets, Lies, Gizmos,
and Spies**
Abrams
Disappearing ink,
wooden horses,
James Bond and more

Dorros, Arthur
Under the Sun
Amulet
Ehmet crossing Bosnia
to find safety

Fleischman, Paul
**Dateline: Troy, new
updated edition**
Candlewick
Ancient and modern
worlds-not so different

Foerstel, Herbert N.
Killing the Messenger
Praeger
The risky business
of journalism

Friedman, Devin and
the Editors of GQ
This is Our War
Artistan
War in Iraq through
soldiers' cameras

Halilbegovic, Nadja
My Childhood Under Fire
Kids Can
Keeping a diary in
war-torn Sarajevo

Haney, Eric L.
Inside Delta Force
Delacorte
Nameless heroes in
the war on terrorism

Hendrex, Daniel with
Wes Smith
A Soldier's Promise
*Simon Spotlight
Entertainment*
Jamil, an Iraqi teen's
journey to America

Kopelman, Jay with
Melinda Roth
From Baghdad, With Love
The Lyons Press
A Marine, the war, and
a dog named Lava

Némirovsky, Irène
Suite Francaise
Knopf
Life and death in
occupied France

Riverbend
Baghdad Burning II
The Feminist Press
The war through the
eyes of a girl blogger

Salbi, Zainab
Other Side of War
National Geographic
Women's stories
worldwide

Book Excerpt:
How can we talk about
war without talking about
its sounds? War is not
just gunfire or explosions,
but a dissonant concert:
a flock of birds screeching
in the night, a stranger
breathing in your ear,
the sound of your child
pleading. Even worse, i
t is silence of children so
terrorized they do not
scream, or the silence of
your own guilty prayer
of thanks that it was not
your children who died.
War, says a friend of
mine, is not about sound
at all, but about silence.
The silence of humanity.

Sauro, Christy W., Jr.
The Twins Platoon
Zenith Press
1967, young Marines
in Vietnam

Sedgwick, Marcus
The Foreshadowing
Wendy Lamb
Sasha racing across
1915 France to save
her brother

Shugaar, Antony
I Lie for a Living
National Geographic
Spies through the ages

Slade, Arthur
Megiddo's Shadow
Wendy Lamb
Edward, fighting Turks
in Palestine in WWI

Springer, Jane
Genocide
Groundwood
The ultimate crime
against humanity

Weisskopf, Michael
Blood Brothers
Henry Holt
18 months on an
amputee ward

express yourself!

create, compose, dream, imagine, perform

DIY

Bruce, Stephen
Serendipity Sundaes
Universe
Icy desserts to cool the mind

Carle, Megan and Jill Carle with Judi Carle
Teens Cook Dessert
Ten Speed
Sweet treats, mouthwatering recipes

Dunnington, Rose
Big Snacks, Little Meals
Lark
Fun eats, after school, dinnertime, anytime

Gaines, Thom
Digital Photo Madness
Lark
Weird and wacky images created with cameras

Howell, Vickie
Not Another Teen Knitting Book
Sterling
Project for goths, girly-girls, skaters, punks and nerds

Nguyen, Duy
Origami Birds
Sterling
Paper art of flight

Nicolay, Megan
Generation T
Workman
108 ways to transform a T-shirt

Okey, Shannon
Knitgrrl 2
Watson-Guptill
16 new patterns for hip knitters

Raymond, Carole
Student's Go Vegan Cookbook
Three Rivers
Easy, cheap vegetarian recipes

Scott, Damion and Kris Ex
How to Draw Hip-Hop
Watson-Guptill
Edgy, funky, rap life, comic art

Stern, Sam
Cooking Up a Storm
Candlewick
A teen survival cookbook

Todd, Mark and Esther Pearl Watson
Whatcha Mean, What's a Zine?
Graphia
A guide: mini-comics, hand-made magazines

Ure, Susan
The Altered Book Scrapbook
Sterling/Chapelle
Recycled books become readable art

Yamamoto, Neal
Superhero Explosion
Impact
Amazing comics, 60 easy steps

Zent, Sheila
Sew Teen
Sixth&Spring
Simple designs for the fashion forward

On Stage/ On Screen

Belli, Mary Lou and Dinah Lenney
Acting for Young Actors
Back Stage
How to develop your craft

Caldwell, Sara
Splatter Flicks
Allworth
Making low-budget horror movies

Collins, Ken and Victor Wishna
In Their Company
Umbrage
Portraits of American playwrights

Fenjves, Pablo F. and Rocky Lang
How I Broke Into Hollywood
ReganBooks
Success secrets from Tinseltown survivors

Fleischman, Sid
Escape!
Greenwillow
The astonishing Harry Houdini

Gresh, Lois H. and Robert Weinberg
The Science of James Bond
Wiley
Technology that made the films fabulous

Levy, David B.
Your Career in Animation
Allworth
Tips for breaking in and surviving

Meason, Christopher and Timothy Shaner, editors
The Art of X-Men: The Last Stand
Newmarket
Bringing superheroes to life on film

Milano, Roy
Monsters
Del Rey
Dracula, Frankenstein, Wolfman and more

Rapp, Anthony
Without You
Simon & Schuster
Theatre life of Rent's star

Romano, Christy Carlson
Grace's Turn
Hyperion
From school show to Broadway dreams

Sanders, James, editor
Scenes from the City
Rizzoli
Our streets as backdrop for movies and TV

Schatz, Howard
In Character
Bulfinch
Emotions revealed on actors' faces

Siegel, Siena Cherson with artwork by Mark Siegel
To Dance
Richard Jackson/ Athenuem
A ballerina's life as graphic novel

Vaz, Mark Cotta
Mythic Vision
Knopf
The making of the film Eragon

Warrick, Karen Clemens
James Dean
Enslow
Brilliant actor who died too young

Poetry: Raps, Rhymes, Rants

Carlson, Lori Marie and Oscar Hijuelos, editors
Burnt Sugar/ Caña Quemada
Free Press
Cuban voices, English and Spanish

Derricotte, Toi, Cornelius Eady, Camille T. Dungy, editors
Gathering Ground
Univ. of Michigan Pr.
From an African American poetry community

Fragos, Emily, editor
The Dance
Knopf
Celebrating motion, energy, emotion

Fry, Stephen
The Ode Less Travelled
Gotham Books
Tools for aspiring poets

Johnson, Linton Kwesi
Mi Revalueshanary Fren
Ausable
Sounds of England via Jamaican creole

Poe, Edgar Allan, illustrations by Ryan Price
The Raven
KCP Poetry
Once upon a midnight dreary...nevermore!

Sappho, translated by Willis Barnstone
Sweetbitter Love
Shambhala
Antiquity's lyric poet in English and Greek

Soto, Gary
A Fire in My Hands, revised and expanded
Harcourt
Everyday wonders of growing up

25

Thayer, Ernest L., illustrations by Joe Morse
Casey at the Bat
KCP Poetry
A cool slugger at play in the city

The Power of Words

Clark, Roy Peter
Writing Tools
Little, Brown
50 ways to build your skills

Freedman, Samuel G.
Letters to a Young Journalist
Basic
Advice from a seasoned professional

Gotera, Amanda Blue, editor
The Best Teen Writing of 2006
Alliance for Young Artists & Writers
Award-winning works from across the U.S.A.

Hole, Georgia
The Real McCoy
Oxford
Why we say the things we say

Miller, Joe
Cross-X
Farrar, Straus & Giroux
Underdog debate team's winning season

Book Excerpt:
"I'm Mrs. Rinehart," she said cheerily, trying to shake off her bad mood. "This is the debate class. You are the beginners. You are the novices. You are the hope for the future. You are the ones who are going to win trophies like this." She gestured toward a handsome copper chalice rising from an old audiovisual cart stuffed with books and papers and plastic cups full of pencils and pens. "We run with the big dogs."

A few of the kids chuckled at this short white woman who stood before them in her prim silk blouse and matching marigold skirt, trying to talk trash.
"We do," she insisted, hands back on her hips.

Orr, Tamra B.
Extraordinary Debates
Franklin Watts
Polish your public speaking

Rominger, Lynne
Extraordinary Blogs And Ezines
Franklin Watts
Express yourself online

Saltz, Ina
Body Type
Abrams Image
Words on flesh

The Soundtrack of Your Life

Beaujon, Andrew
Body Piercing Saved My Life
Da Capo
Inside the phenomenon of Christian Rock

Bono, The Edge, Adam Clayton, Larry Mullen, Jr. with Neil McCormick
U2 by U2
HarperCollins
From Dublin to world domination

Burlingame, Jeff
Kurt Cobain
Enslow
An insider's look of at short, tragic life

Cheshire, Simon
Plastic Fantastic
Delacorte
Pop star/fan: elevator encounter

Collingwood, Jeremy
Bob Marley
Cassell Illustrated
His musical legacy

Crumb, R.
R. Crumb's Heroes of Blues, Jazz & Country
Abrams
Brought to life in vibrant portraits

DeRogatis, Jim
Staring at Sound
Broadway Books
The wonderful weird Flaming Lips

Edwards, Gavin
Is Tiny Dancer Really Elton's Little John?
Three Rivers
Music's mysteries and myths revealed

Frederikse, Tom and Phil Benedictus
How to DJ
St. Martin's Griffin
Insider's guide to success on the decks

Greenwald, Andy
Nothing Feels Good
St. Martin's Griffin
The musical movement called emo

Groleau, Jean-Jacques, Thomas Mahler and Patrick Tchiakpé
Music Game Book
Assouline
Who? What? When? Where? How? Why?

Jordan, Herb
Motown in Love
Pantheon
Lyrics from Detroit's golden era

Joseph, Jamal
Tupac Shakur Legacy
Atria
His words, his image, his soul

Manning, Sarra
Let's Get Lost
Dutton
When Isabel falls for an indie-rocker

Myers, Walter Dean with illustrations by Christopher Myers
Jazz
Holiday House
A celebration with verse and images

Nathan, Amy
Meet the Musicians
Henry Holt
New York Philharmonic players' paths to success

Reynolds, Tom
I Hate Myself and Want to Die
Hyperion
The most depressing songs ever

Sherry, James and Neil Aldis
Heavy Metal Thunder
Chronicle
Cover art that decorated vinyl

Tanner, Mike
Flat-out Rock
Annick
Great bands of the 60s

Trynin, Jen
Everything I'm Cracked Up to Be
Harcourt
To the edge of rock stardom and back down

Zinner, Nicholas
I Hope You Are All Happy Now
St. Martin's Griffin
Inside the world of the Yeah Yeah Yeahs

Vision Becomes Image

Bancroft, Tom
Creating Characters with Personality
Watson-Guptill
Drawing animals, superheroes, zombies

Desnoëttes, Caroline
Look Closer
Walker
Masterpieces examined in detail

Ganz, Nicholas
Graffiti Women
Abrams
Spreading their tags and talents worldwide

Gastman, Roger, Darin Rowland, and Ian Sattler
Freight Train Graffiti
Abrams
Art that travels by rail

Gibson, Jon M.
I Am 8-Bit
Chronicle
Inspired by classic videogames

Govenar, Alan B.
Extraordinary Ordinary People
Candlewick
Keeping traditional techniques alive

Hignite, Todd
In the Studio
Yale Univ. Pr.
Extraordinary possibilities of comic art

Metzner, Jeffrey
Stick
Clarkson Potter
Images reduced to the simplest form

Smith, Anna Deavere
Letters to a Young Artist
Anchor
How to conduct a creative life

Sullivan, George
Berenice Abbott, Photographer
Clarion
Her camera targeting NYC

Waldman, Neil
Out of the Shadows
Boyds Mills
Memories of a Bronx-born artist

Waldrep, Lee W.
Becoming an Architect
Wiley
Charting a career in building design

Waterhouse, Jo and David Penhallow
Concrete to Canvas
Watson-Guptill
Emerging from skateboard culture

science

Brain Food

Benjamin, Arthur and
Michael Shermer
Secrets of Mental Math
Three Rivers
Lightning calculations
and amazing tricks

Cadbury, Deborah
Space Race
HarperCollins
From Sputnik to "The
Eagle has landed"

Darling, David
Gravity's Arc
Wiley
The cause of the
apple's fall

Fisher, Adrian
**The Amazing Book
of Mazes**
Abrams
Guided tour of a timeless
art form

Fradin, Dennis Brindell
With a Little Luck
Dutton
Good fortune helped
great discoveries

Gore, Al
An Inconvenient Truth
Rodale
The hard science of
global warming

Hill, Steele and
Michael Carlowicz
The Sun
Abrams
Colorful story of our
nearest star

Hooper, Dan
Dark Cosmos
Collins
A crash course in particle
physics

Langone, John, Bruce
Stutz and Andrea
Gianopoulos
Theories for Everything
National Geographic
From the heavens to Z
particles

Nemiroff, Robert J.
The Universe
Abrams
365 views of the cosmos

Raymo, Chet
Walking Zero
Walker
The prime meridian
and science history

Seckel, Al
Optical Illusions
Firefly
When seeing isn't
believing

Stewart, Ian
**Letters to a Young
Mathematician**
Basic
Insight into the
numbers game

Fur, Feathers, Fins and Scales

Anderson, Allen and
Linda Anderson
Rescued
New World Library
Saving pets from
Hurricane Katrina

Buono, Vito
Dogs
White Star
Visual guide to our
faithful companions

Cox, Lynne
Grayson
Knopf
Swimming the Pacific to
save a baby whale

> **Book Excerpt:**
> At first it seemed to be
> a whisper, then it grew
> louder, steadily like
> someone trying to shout
> for help but unable to
> get the words out. I kept
> swimming and trying
> to figure out what was
> happening.
> The sound changed.
> It became stranger like
> the end of a scream.

Ehrich, Joanne, editor
Koalas
Koala Jo
Portraits of the shy,
serene marsupial

Eldredge, Kate with Debra
M. Eldredge
Head of the Class
Howell
Woof, woof: tips from a
teen expert

Haines, Tim and Paul
Chambers
**The Complete Guide to
Prehistoric Life**
Firefly
A who's what of the
ancient world

Marrin, Albert
Saving the Buffalo
Scholastic Nonfiction
From the brink of
extinction

Martin, Gilles and
Myriam Baran
Butterflies of the World
Abrams
Brilliantly colored,
endlessly fascinating

Noyes, Deborah
One Kingdom
Houghton Mifflin
The bond between
humans and animals

Owens, Mark and
Delia Owens
Secrets of the Savanna
Houghton Mifflin
Saving elephants from
poachers

Payton, Brian
Shadow of the Bear
Bloomsbury
Majestic animals,
endangered species

Turpin, Tom
**Flies in the Face of
Fashion, Mites Make
Right, and Other
Bugdacious Tales**
Purdue Univ.
Increase your insect
intelligence

Witherington, Blair
Sea Turtles
Voyageur
Ancient and elegant
mariners

action! adventure!

Sports

Atlas, Teddy with
Peter Alson
Atlas
Ecco
From Rikers Island to
the boxing ring

Belth, Alex
Stepping Up
Persea
Curt Flood: the baseball
player who stood up to
the Major League

Carter, Alden R.
**Love, Football, and
Other Contact Sports**
Holiday House
Players, their fans and the
girls who love them

Cuadros, Paul
A Home on the Field
Rayo
Mexican-American teen
soccer champs in small
town U.S.A.

Fagone, Jason
**Horsemen of the
Esophagus**
Crown
Inside the belly of the
competitive eating beast

Fitzgerald, Dawn
Soccer Chick Rules
Deborah Brodie
Tess' all-girl team lining
up for the goal

Gifford, Clive
**The Kingfisher Soccer
Encyclopedia**
Kingfisher
The game, the rules, the
history, the champs

Lewis, Michael
The Blind Side
Norton
Finding a voice on the
football field

Lipsyte, Robert
Heroes of Baseball
Atheneum
From Ty Cobb to Ichiro
Suzuki

Lipsyte, Robert
Raiders Night
HarperTempest
Matt, ascending the
throne of football royalty

Lupica, Mike
Heat
Philomel
From a backyard in Cuba
to Yankee Stadium

Macy, Sue
Freeze Frame
National Geographic
Snow, ice, skates, sleds,
ski: The Winter Olympics

Murdock, Catherine
Gilbert
Dairy Queen
Houghton Mifflin
DJ: the girl trying out for
the football team

National Basketball
Association
The Perfect Team
Doubleday
Building the best to take
the court

Paur, Jason with photos
by Corey Rich
My Favorite Place
Chronicle
Athletes exploring the
great outdoors

Rich, Sue
The Tennis Handbook
Three Rivers
The forehand, the
backhand, the history
and more

Ritter, John H.
Under the Baseball Moon
Philomel
When Glory Martinez
came back to town

Russo, Christopher and
Allen St.John
**The Mad Dog Hall of
Fame**
Doubleday
Athletes, teams, coaches,
venues...

Saraiva, Dave
The Brushback Report
Ballantine
Spoofs and goofs of the
sporting world

Silver, Michael with
Natalie Coughlin
Golden Girl
Rodale
Backstroking her way to
Olympic gold

Thrasher Magazine
Skate and Destroy
Universe
Ollies, oops, tats, boards
and bruises

Vecsey, George
Baseball
Modern Library
A history of America's
grand old game

Villareal, Ray
**My Father, the Angel
of Death**
Piñata
Jesse's dad, the cloaked
wrestling champ

Walters, Guy
Berlin Games
William Morrow
Olympics, 1936: politics
and personality in Nazi
Germany

Zweig, Eric
Home Plate Don't Move
Firefly
Bat men and mound men,
off-the-cuff

Mad Action: Escapes, Espionage, Intrigue

Cole, Stephen
Thieves Like Us
Bloomsbury
Nefarious teen dream
team

Gross, Philip
The Lastling
Clarion
Saving the Yeti: the last
of her kind

Hokenson, Terry
The Winter Road
Front Street
Willa: surviving the
Canadian wilderness

**Book Excerpt
(Heroes of Baseball):**
Some of our heroes of the
game were also great
human beings. Jackie
Robinson and Curt Flood
were heroes who stood
up for their principles and
not only made baseball a
better game, but America
a better place. Some of
them had tremendous
positive impact on others.
Babe Ruth, a throwaway
kid, was an enormous
inspiration to an America
of struggling immigrants.
Mickey Mantle played
hard despite a painful
bone disease in his legs,
and as he was dying in
1995, became an
eloquent spokesman for
organ donation.
   Of course, not all the
great players were great
people. Some were
ordinary guys with
extraordinary talents, and
some had human flaws
that disappointed us.
Pete Rose gambled on his
own games, which made
fans wonder about the
honesty of those games,
and a number of players
have used illegal drugs to
enhance their skills,
which is unfair to those
who want to play clean.
   And then there was
Ty Cobb, a vicious, loud-
mouthed bully. Hardly
anyone liked him. Even
his own teammates kept
their distance, afraid he'd
explode, scream at them,
even punch them out. So
how could he be one of
my heroes of baseball?

Book Excerpt:
She came shooting off
the wall like a human
torpedo, gliding through
the water with cold,
relentless precision.
Unleashing her incompa-
rable, undulating dolphin
kicks, Natalie Coughlin
began to pull away from
the field in the 100-meter
backstroke, popping to
the surface nearly a body
length ahead of her
closest pursuer. From that
prime vantage point—
with a picturesque view
of the Athens sunset, a
mere 35 meters between
her and redemption—
Coughlin was as good
as gold.

Horowitz, Anthony
Ark Angel
Philomel
Alex Rider: babysitter?

Just My Opinion!
It [Ark Angel] was Book Six of the Alex Rider series and I wanted to find out what new adventure he was going on and to see if he lived. Anthony Horowitz is a detailed writer, so reading this book was fun. I saw it as a movie as I read it. I recommend all of the books in the Alex Rider series.
Teen Reviewer:
Christine Keappock
Parkchester Branch
Library, Bronx

Lopez, Jack
In the Break
Little, Brown
Love, hate and the power of the sea

Marks, Graham
Missing in Tokyo
Bloomsbury
Adam and Aiko prowling the underworld

McNab, Andy and
Robert Rigby
Payback
Putnam's
Danny and Gramps:
retired spies

Sachar, Louis
Small Steps
Delacorte
Armpit: turning his life around again

Just My Opinion!
Small Steps is about a boy named Theodore a.k.a. Armpit. He was once at Camp Green Lake, which is a juvenile center. Armpit has been at Camp Green Lake for two years and is on the right track, going to school and staying out of trouble. One of Armpit's old friends from the juvenile center named X-Ray contacts Armpit with a money-making plan to sell tickets for the pop sensation Kaira DeLeon. Now all down-hill things start to happen to Theodore because of some counterfeit tickets. I like this book because of the characters and it is very interesting.
Teen Reviewer:
Steven Osofsky
West New Brighton
Branch Library,
Staten Island

Real Life to the Extreme

Blair, Margaret Whitman
The Roaring Twenty
National Geographic
Women pilots flying 2800 miles cross-country

Johnson, Dolores
Onward
National Geographic
Matthew Henson, enticed by the lure of the Arctic

Norton, Trevor
Underwater to Get Out of the Rain
Da Capo
Exploring marine life from corals to caverns

Parrado, Nando with
Vince Rause
Miracle in the Andes
Crown
72 fearful days on a mountain glacier

Book Excerpt:
"You have been unconscious for three days," he said, with no emotion in his voice. "We had given up on you."
These words made no sense. "What happened to me?" I asked, "Why is it so cold?"
"Do you understand me, Nando?" said Roberto. "We crashed into the mountains. The airplane crashed. We are stranded here."
I shook my head feebly in confusion, or denial, but I could not deny for long what was happening around me. I heard soft moans and sudden cries of pain, and I began to understand that these were the sounds of other people suffering.

Revkin, Andrew C.
The North Pole Was Here
Kingfisher
Artic adventures, unearthing the mysteries

Sandler, Martin W.
Trapped in Ice!
Scholastic Nonfiction
1871, lost whalers, a desperate search

Viesturs, Ed with
David Roberts
No Shortcuts to the Top
Broadway
Mountain climbing, Mt. Rainer to the Himalayas

Willems, Mo
You Can Never Find a Rickshaw When It Monsoons
Hyperion Paperbacks
The world on one cartoon a day

Bronx

Allerton Branch
2740 Barnes Avenue,
10467
718.881.4240

Baychester Branch
2049 Asch Loop North,
10475
718.379.6700

Belmont Branch
610 East 186th Street,
10458
718.933.6410

Bronx Library Center
310 East Kingsbridge
Road,
10458
718.579.4244
TTY: 718.579.4244

Castle Hill Branch
947 Castle Hill Avenue,
10473
718.824.3838

City Island Branch
320 City Island Avenue,
10464
718.885.1703

Clason's Point Branch
1215 Morrison Avenue,
10472
718.842.1235

Eastchester Branch
1385 East Gun Hill Road,
10469
718.653.3292

Edenwald Branch
1255 East 233rd Street,
10466
718.798.3355

Francis Martin Branch
2150 University Avenue,
10453
718.295.5287

Grand Concourse Branch
155 East 173rd Street,
10457
718.583.6611

High Bridge Branch
78 West 168th Street,
10452
718.293.7800

Hunt's Point Branch
877 Southern Boulevard,
10459
718.617.0338

Jerome Park Branch
118 Eames Place,
10468
718.549.5200
(Closed for major
renovations–call for
information)

Kingsbridge Branch
280 West 231st Street,
10463
718.548.5656

Melrose Branch
910 Morris Avenue,
10451
718.588.0110

Morris Park Branch
985 Morris Park Avenue,
10462
718.931.0636

Morrisania Branch
610 East 169th Street,
10456
718.589.9268

Mosholu Branch
285 East 205th Street,
10467
718.882.8239

Mott Haven Branch
321 East 140th Street,
10454
718.665.4878

Parkchester Branch
1985 Westchester
Avenue,
10462
718.829.7830

Pelham Bay Branch
3060 Middletown Road,
10461
718.792.6744

Riverdale Branch
5540 Mosholu Avenue,
10471
718.549.1212

Sedgwick Branch
1701 Martin Luther King,
Jr. Boulevard,
10453
718.731.2074

Soundview Branch
660 Soundview Avenue,
10473
718.589.0880

Spuyten Duyvil Branch
650 West 235th Street,
10463
718.796.1202

Throg's Neck Branch
3025 Cross Bronx
Expressway
Extension,
10465
718.792.2612

Tremont Branch
1866 Washington Avenue,
10457
718.299.5177

Van Cortlandt Branch
3874 Sedgwick Avenue,
10463
718.543.5150

Van Nest Branch
2147 Barnes Avenue,
10462
718.829.5864

Wakefield Branch
4100 Lowerre Place,
10466
718.652.4663

West Farms Branch
2085 Honeywell Avenue,
10460
718.367.5376

**Westchester Square
Branch**
2521 Glebe Avenue.
10461
718.863.0436

**Woodlawn Heights
Branch**
4355 Katonah Avenue,
10470
718.519.9627

Woodstock Branch
761 East 160th Street,
10456
718.665.6255

Manhattan

58th Street Branch
127 East 58th Street,
10022
212.759.7358

67th Street Branch
328 East 67th Street,
10021
212.734.1717
TTY: 212.794.3854

96th Street Branch
112 East 96th Street,
10128
212.289.0908

115th Street Branch
203 West 115th Street,
10026
212.666.9393

125th Street Branch
224 East 125th Street,
10035
212.534.5050

Aguilar Branch
174 East 110th Street,
10029
212.534.2930

**Andrew Heiskell Braille
& Talking Book Library**
40 West 20th Street,
10011
212.206.5400
TTY: 212.206.5458

Bloomingdale Branch
150 West 100th Street,
10025
212.222.8030

Chatham Square Branch
33 East Broadway,
10002
212.964.6598

Columbus Branch
742 10th Avenue,
10019
212.586.5098

Countee Cullen Branch
104 West 136th Street,
10030
212.491.2070

30

Donnell Library Center
20 West 53rd Street,
10019
212.621.0618
TTY: 212.621.0560

**Early Childhood
Resource &
Information Center**
66 Leroy Street,
10014
212.929.0815

Epiphany Branch
228 East 23rd Street,
10010
212.679.2645

Fort Washington Branch
535 West 179th Street,
10033
212.927.3533

George Bruce Branch
518 West 125th Street,
10027
212.662.9727

**Hamilton Fish Park
Branch**
415 East Houston Street,
10002
212.673.2290

Hamilton Grange Branch
503 West 145th Street,
10031
212.926.2147

Harlem Branch
9 West 124th Street,
10027
212.348.5620

Hudson Park Branch
66 Leroy Street,
10014
212.243.6876

**Humanities and Social
Sciences Library**
Fifth Avenue and
42nd Street,
10018
212.930.0830

Inwood Branch
4790 Broadway,
10034
212.942.2445

Jefferson Market Branch
425 Avenue of the
Americas,
10011
212.243.4334

Kips Bay Branch
466 Third Avenue,
10016
212.683.2520

Macomb's Bridge Branch
2650 Adam Clayton
Powell, Jr. Boulevard,
10039
212.281.4900

Mid-Manhattan Library
455 Fifth Avenue,
10016
212.340.0849
TTY: 212.340.0931

Morningside Heights
2900 Broadway,
10025
212.864.2530

Muhlenberg Branch
209 West 23rd Street,
10011
212.924.1585

**Nathan Straus
Teen Central**
20 West 53rd Street,
10019
212.621.0633

New Amsterdam Branch
9 Murray Street,
10007
212.732.8186

**The New York
Public Library for the
Performing Arts**
40 Lincoln Center Plaza,
10023
212.870.1630

Ottendorfer Branch
135 Second Avenue,
10003
212.674.0947

Riverside Branch
127 Amsterdam Avenue,
10023
212.870.1810

Roosevelt Island Branch
524 Main Street, 10044
212.308.6243

St. Agnes Branch
444 Amsterdam Avenue,
10024
212.877.4380

**Schomburg Center for
Research in Black Culture**
515 Malcolm X Boulevard,
10037
212.491.2200

**Science, Industry and
Business Library (SIBL)**
188 Madison Avenue,
10016
212.592.7000

Seward Park Branch
192 East Broadway,
10002
212.477.6770

**Terence Cardinal Cooke-
Cathedral Branch**
560 Lexington Avenue,
10022
212.752.3824

Tompkins Square Branch
331 East 10th Street,
10009
212.228.4747

**Washington Heights
Branch**
1000 St. Nicholas Avenue,
10032
212.923.6054

Webster Branch
1465 York Avenue,
10021
212.288.5049

Yorkville Branch
222 East 79th Street,
10021
212.744.5824

Staten Island

Dongan Hills Branch
1617 Richmond Road,
10304
718.351.1444

Great Kills Branch
56 Giffords Lane,
10308
718.984.6670

Huguenot Park Branch
830 Huguenot Avenue,
10312
718.984.4636

New Drop Branch
309 New Drop Lane,
10306
718.351.2977

Port Richmond Branch
75 Bennett Street,
10302
718.442.0158

Richmondtown Branch
200 Clarke Avenue,
10306
718.668.0413

St. George Library Center
5 Central Avenue,
10301
718.442.8560
TTY: 718.733.4315

South Beach Branch
21-25 Robin Road,
10305
718.816.5834

Stapleton Branch
132 Canal Street,
10304
718.727.0427

**Todt Hill-Westerleigh
Branch**
2550 Victory Boulevard,
10314
718.494.1642

Tottenville Branch
7430 Amboy Road,
10307
718.984.0945

**West New Brighton
Branch**
976 Castleton Avenue,
10310
718.442.1416

Ordering Information

Books for the Teen Age is published each year in March by the Office of Young Adult Services. Copies cost ten dollars ($10.00) each. On mail orders there is a charge for mailing and handling:
1 copy: $1.00
2 to 5 copies: $1.25
bulk orders: $1.50

Order from:
Office of Collections and Services
The New York
Public Library
455 Fifth Avenue
New York, NY 10016
212.340.0912

For additional information:
212.340.0907
teenlink@nypl.org

Special Thanks!

Special thanks are extended to The New York Public Library's Young Adult Librarians who served as committee members and who, throughout the year, recommend selections for *Books for the Teen Age*.

Liana Acevedo
Jay Barksdale
Jenny Baum
Agnes Beck-Statile
Debra Behr
Ann-Marie Braithwaite
Shauntee Burns
Susan Buttaccio
Clivel Charlton
Amy Chow
Sarah Couri
Jeremy Czerw
Chris DeCostanza
Beryl Eber
Jenny Engstrom
John Fahs
Elizabeth Fineberg
Valerie Floridia
Lisa Gaona
Nancy Hampton
Marie Hansen
Verna Hodge
Celia Holm
Megan Honig
Steven Horvath
James Huffman
Gloria Hughes
Shelley Huntington
Melissa Jenvey
Patrelle Johnson
Cara v. W. Kinsey
Lauren Lazar

Johanna Lewis
Andrea Lipinski
Veronica Marinescu
H. Jack Martin
Towanda Mathurin
Eric McCarthy
Abigail Meisterman
Yajaira Mejia
Lynda Perez
Kimberly Reid
Joanne Rosario
Nicole Rosenbluth-Whitman
Anne Rouyer
Lindsy Serrano
Christopher Shoemaker
Karlan Sick
Victor Simmons Jr.
Caryl Soriano
Sandra Trachte
Emily Valente
Anne Marie Witte
Laurence Yamazaki
Robyn Zaneski